THE MARRIAGE ARK

Endorsements

"Engaged and longtime married couples alike will be blessed by *The Marriage Ark*. Through scripture, wisdom and transparency, Margaret shines light on God's instructions for marital success. In this day and age, I cannot think of a more timely or more needed book than *The Marriage Ark*!"

—**Barbara Mandrell**, Award-winning Country Artist

"For anyone who desperately needs or desires a deeper level of intimacy in marriage, *The Marriage Ark* is a lifesaver! Margaret Phillips provides no-nonsense advice and uncompromising truth that will help heal the "holes in your soul." Rather than pie-in-the-sky platitudes, Margaret leads you to discover fresh, practical ideas that you can put to use right now. I have greatly benefitted from Margaret's insights and I am confident that you will, too!"

—**Ken Abraham**, *New York Times* Bestselling Author

"With wit, insight, home spun stories, and a wealth of experience, Margaret Phillips, weaves a tapestry that would fit well into any home. Do you need help in communication in your marriage? Do you grasp and enjoy the differences in the Master's plan in making them "male and female?" Do you need a road map to help you navigate your family back into wholeness and health? Then as someone who has benefited from the skillful guidance and clarity of teaching from Margaret Phillips, it is my honor to commend to you *The Marriage Ark* as part of your communication prescription."

—**Dr. James W Goll**, Founder of God Encounters, Best Selling Author, Life Language Coach

"We have witnessed many people who have created strategies for career and financial success. But those same people frequently have no plan for success in their marriage. In *The Marriage Ark*. Margaret shares a clear blueprint for being as intentional about success in your marriage as you would expect in business. With no plan in place, your ark—and your marriage—will likely sink. Don't take that chance."

—**Dan and Joanne Miller**, 48days.com,
Authors and Coaches

"The allegory of marriage being an Ark floating above the greatest storm in the history of the world is timely as well as accurate. Never before has family and marriage been under the attack it is now. Family is the superstructure of society and the union between husband and wife is the bond of agreement. I highly recommend this book for married couples, counselors, pastors, and people considering being married. Also, it's never too late to repair a marriage and it certainly is worth it."

—**Mickey Robinson**, Pastor,
International Speaker, Author

"Margaret was instrumental in helping my wife and I to navigate through the early years of our marriage when we were overwhelmed with conflict, pain from buried trauma and toxic patterns of relating. Many of the principles she shares in *The Marriage Ark* gave us a foundation to learn **how to love** by applying biblical principles and to rely on God to guide us. This book is a great first-step book for couples facing rough seas."

—**Mark Alt**, Lead Pastor, The Bridge Church

"When my friend, Margaret Phillips, speaks, I've learned to sit up and take notes. She is a storehouse of wisdom. In *The Marriage Ark*, she zeros in on marriage and shows us how to build a safe place to ride out the storms of married life. She also shows us how to make the most of the journey while we're in there. Regardless of whether you're just setting-sail on a new life with someone, find yourself drowning in the middle of a hurricane, or wanting to deepen and enrich a long-term marriage, this book is for you."

—**Gail Hyatt**, Mentor, Artist, and
Wife of Author Michael Hyatt

THE
MARRIAGE
ARK

Securing Your Marriage
in a Sea of Uncertainty

MARGARET PHILLIPS

NASHVILLE

NEW YORK • MELBOURNE • VANCOUVER

THE MARRIAGE ARK
Securing Your Marriage in a Sea of Uncertainty

© 2017 MARGARET PHILLIPS

Published in New York, New York, by Morgan James Publishing. Morgan James is a trademarks of Morgan James, LLC. www.MorganJamesPublishing.com

The Morgan James Speakers Group can bring authors to your live event. For more information or to book an event visit The Morgan James Speakers Group at www.TheMorganJamesSpeakersGroup.com.

All scripture quotations, unless otherwise noted, are taken from The New King James Version. Copyright 1997 by Thomas Nelson, Inc.

ISBN 978-1-68350-307-1 paperback
ISBN 978-1-68350-309-5 eBook
ISBN 978-1-68350-308-8 hardcover
Library of Congress Control Number: 2016917110

Edited by:
Christy M. Nunez

Cover Design by:
Rachel Lopez
www.r2cdesign.com

Interior Design by:
Bonnie Bushman
The Whole Caboodle Graphic Design

In an effort to support local communities, raise awareness and funds, Morgan James Publishing donates a percentage of all book sales for the life of each book to Habitat for Humanity Peninsula and Greater Williamsburg.

Get involved today! Visit
www.MorganJamesBuilds.com

To my husband Gary,
Thank you for your deep love and commitment
in building our amazing Marriage Ark

Table of Contents

Foreword

Not long ago, I was doing a book signing at an event where I had spoken. I was having a great time talking with the folks in line, but my conversation with one lady really sticks out in my mind.

I'd said something during my talk about the relationship between marriage and money, and she wanted to tell me her story. But when she said she and her husband had been married for 30 years without a single fight, I was skeptical.

Okay, so I was little *more* than skeptical. And I told her so.

"I don't buy it," I said.

Now, I wasn't trying to be rude. I was just trying to be real. Anyone who's been married for longer than 20 minutes knows that two people don't live together that long without a hint of conflict. Human beings simply aren't wired to agree about everything all the time—and that's okay.

One of the awesome things about God is the way He created us as unique people. We're all made in His image, but we're also individuals. Saying "I do" doesn't change that. Fortunately, those differences usually make us stronger. If I'm weak in one area, my wife, Sharon, can fill in the gaps—and I do the same for her.

So, different is good. As my friend, the late Larry Burkett used to say, "If two people just alike get married, one of you is unnecessary."

The problem is, sometimes those differences erupt at the most stressful times of our lives. When those storms hit, even the best of marriages need some coaching. They need a safe place until the storms pass.

I speak from personal experience.

I've been married to a wonderful, godly woman for almost 35 years. I mean, when I read the Proverbs 31 definition of a virtuous wife—"her worth is far above rubies and the heart of her husband safely trusts in her, and he will have no lack of gain"—I automatically think of Sharon. To me, no one lives that out better than she does.

But you know what they say: Opposites attract. That may not be true every time, but it definitely was for us. Those differences that brought us together, though, almost tore us apart at the seams.

About 10 years into our marriage, we almost hit the breaking point. We had been working our way out of bankruptcy for three years, and the stress was really taking its toll. That's actually not unusual; money fights are consistently one the leading causes of divorce. But I've also learned that, most of the time, money troubles are just a symptom of deeper cracks in the relationship.

For us, those cracks included a lack of confidence and a lack of trust. We loved each other deeply, but the genuine, raw terror that we were experiencing on a daily basis was having a negative impact on our lives and our marriage.

It felt like we were fighting to keep our heads above water in the middle of an overwhelming flood. Thankfully, God led to us to someone who helped us get back on solid ground.

That person was Margaret Phillips.

Over time, Margaret pointed us back to God's plan for our marriage. The counseling she provided was one of the major reasons Sharon and I were able to stay together through the aftermath of the bankruptcy. Even after we had regained our footing and started experiencing success again, Margaret's insights helped us navigate the choppy waters of living in the public eye.

I'm thankful for many of the things Sharon and I learned from Margaret, but one of the things I'm most thankful for is a habit we're still practicing today: our morning meetings on the deck.

Sharon and I are both very task-oriented people with incredibly busy schedules. But our spirits really come together when we tackle things that need to be done and issues that need to be decided.

That usually happens during our time together each morning. Every day at 5 a.m., we spend time reflecting on Scripture and praying over our day. For us, there's nothing better than spending time with God and each other as we sit on our deck and watch the sun come up over the Tennessee hills.

It's become a sacred time for us.

As I said, that's just one of the great things we've learned from Margaret. In fact, it's hard to quantify just how much of an impact she has had on the Ramsey family over the years.

It's not a stretch to say that Margaret helped save our marriage, and we're just one of the thousands of couples she's helped. Whether your marriage is facing an overwhelming storm or just needing to find a little better footing, I believe Margaret can help you too.

—**Dave Ramsey**
July 15, 2016

Preface

The Marriage Ark was birthed from a place of longing to see strong bonds, faithfulness, and a true Edenic experience in marriages today. It was a deep search to find the actual building blocks that could and would ensure a safe shelter, a refuge for couples. My husband and I had to intentionally discover these at each new phase and each new storm that came our way.

As a young woman, I fantasized about my husband and the family I hoped to have one day. I married at 19-years-old and began the reality of that dream. Over and over, as the reality of life came crashing like waves, some gently rocking our boat, others thrashing, we both had to discover the tools to build an enduring vessel. I will say, unabashedly, all that was with the help of our God.

This book is being completed as I mark my 30th year as a licensed marriage and family therapist. I majored in psychology at a university only because I loved the science of it, not having a vision for its use as a vocation. My vision was to be a wife and mother. After having our babies, two of whom were born on the mission field in West Africa, and mothering through the early childhood years, another vision emerged. My husband was a minister and we were met with difficult marital situations over and over.

The yearning to be able to make a difference began to grow. Out of that was born the years of going back to graduate school, a year-long internship, and two more years in a family systems institute. These were grueling years tooling myself to work in the field and in the trenches. My passion for couples has only grown and multiplied through this work. The pain of divorce is wrenching. The prices are enormous.

So day by day, I sit with couples and individuals, who have taught me so much about the human fabric woven together by our Creator: the tenacity, the deep desires, the resilience, the weaknesses, and the strengths. I have so much honor and gratitude for these people who have bared their souls with me. I have sought through *The Marriage Ark* to share the hope and wisdom of God's blueprint for healthy relationships, enduring and fulfilling ones that can last a lifetime.

—Margaret Arrowood Phillips
August 1, 2016

Acknowledgements

The Marriage Ark originated as a study I wrote to fit into a Sunday School format. Dr. Al Morris from Eastern Kentucky University did the editing on that project. He was invaluable in the early forming of the course. My daughter-in-law, Amy Phillips spent many hours turning my writing into a usable notebook. We taught this class for 8 years and had mentors such as Herman and Patsy Partin and Harold and Robin Madison come alongside us, serving as teachers and mentors for small groups.

Three years ago, I asked Joanne Miller and Vicki Shaub to join me in forming a support group for writers, painters, and musicians who wanted to grow in their form of art. This group was called The Creatives. Inspired by these women, I resolved to turn this manuscript into a book.

I can't thank Christy Nunez enough for accepting the role of editor to help me transition the study guides into a book. Her wisdom, expertise, and hard work kept me on track to cross the finish line.

My sincerest gratitude goes to all the couples who have passed through my office the past 30 years. They have taught me and continually inspired me with their courage, their perseverance, and their creative efforts toward the care and feeding of the marriage relationship.

And my sincerest love and thankfulness to my dad, Gene Arrowood, and my dear stepmother Lorene Arrowood, whom we lost in 2016, for their constant championing of my efforts. To my husband, Gary, there are no words to describe the anchor you are for everything I do: the love, patience, forbearance, and servant-heart you bring as my ark-mate. Also, our sons Joshua, Matthew, and Micah and their families, have served as plumb lines for building safe arks in this present culture.

Introduction

The quest for intimacy, strong bonds, and all that relationships can be is a quest in my own life that has spilled into my life's work of helping others. As a child, I have precious memories of my mom and dad hugging and kissing. I would wriggle my little body between them to get in on the action! They would lift me up and we'd all hug and kiss. I felt loved and safely cocooned between them. This sowed the seeds of expectation in my heart for the experience I long for others to have in relationships and family.

On my mother's side of the family, there was great anticipation of going to Grandma and Pa Coffey's home. Aunts, uncles, and grandparents would meet me there with love filling the rooms, beautiful lush flowers in the gardens, and chocolate ice cream in the freezer. At Pa Gurney's house, on my father's side, I could always count on hearty laughter, 6-layer homemade applesauce cake, and an empty lap just waiting for me.

My happy memories of the family were brought to an abrupt halt when doctors discovered my mother's terminal cancer. She was 32-years-old and I only ten. The cancer went on a deadly rampage in her body; treatments were powerless. Tears and sorrow filled our home, with a foreboding cloud hanging overhead. Her premature death, followed by the untimely passing of my aunt, my mother's young sister-in-law a short six months later from Hodgkin's disease pierced through us all.

My vibrant, red-headed grandmother spiraled into an extreme depression. The family could no longer tolerate the painful togetherness of Christmas and other holidays because it magnified who was not, and would never again, be with us.

So, somewhere deep inside me, there has been a driving force for rekindling the greatest possible relationship in the way of family. Having been married for almost five decades, being blessed with biological sons, God-given daughters-in-law, and more grandchildren than I could have ever imagined, (13 to date), I am more convinced than ever that God had a marvelous idea when he conceived of marriage and family.

Family starts with a man and a woman coming together to form a third entity called a marriage. Nothing is potentially more beautiful and satisfying and answers the calls of our deepest longings. It is not good for man to be alone.

Mary Pipher in *The Shelter of Each Other: Rebuilding Our Families*, says "our culture is at war with families," (1996). Economic pressures, the proliferation of addiction of every sort, and couples living in geographical distance from extended-family support, are just a few of the factors contributing to the stressors on the family today.

I have given much of my life to my work as a marriage and family therapist, not only because I deeply believe in the beauty and holiness of this union, but also for the sake of the children left behind in the ravages of divorce. I am the product of a broken home, and even though mine was broken through death, I know the tear in a child's heart caused by losing the family as they knew it.

The Marriage Ark is a vehicle to be used one of two ways: You can either begin building a marriage ark that will shelter and keep you safe in the midst of storms; or you can survey the ark you are in for repairs needed to ensure your relationship can stand firm against the elements. Building a shelter takes planning, time, and hard work. We have been given the blueprint as surely as Noah was. The effort is entirely worth it, for this is the place of safety, love, family, and ultimately salvation.

"But I will establish My covenant with you; and you shall go into the ark – you, your sons, your wife, and your sons' wives with you,"
(Genesis 6:18).

CHAPTER 1

Building Your Ark: On Rock or Sand?

"Unless the Lord builds the house, they labor in vain who build it,"

(Psalms 127:1).

H ello. This is Margaret Phillips." Silence on the other end, followed by sounds of crying. "I'm sorry. My husband was sleeping last night and his phone buzzed at 2:00 a.m. and I automatically reached for it, and it read, 'Hey babe, just got off the flight. Can't wait to see you.' I got up and began searching his phone and emails and he's been in an affair at least 18 months. I don't know what to do. I feel like I am drowning. Do you have anything open at all, any time you can see me?"

I can't begin to count the times I have heard these words. Also the calls that begin: "We need help. I don't know what happened. We barely talk anymore. We are so far apart I don't know if we can ever get back." Or "My wife is coming in from work every night and starts pouring herself some wine and it continues until she falls in the bed. I hate to think this, but I believe she is becoming an alcoholic." The scenarios are endless.

Fierce winds blow. Waves crash. Seas roar. Relationships unravel. The sails tear. In fact, there are gaping holes in the sails. They are tattered. These phone calls represent bruised and battered and broken hearts. Real people and real tears. Gut wrenching losses and even if repair takes place, the toll is greater than I can put into words. For a long time, I have considered myself a midwife to pain and tears. And a surgeon. And a part of the healing community.

Building Your Ark: On Rock or Sand?

I admit Noah might sound a little outdated, but to me he is one of the most relevant icons in scripture. He actually did save his large family in the midst of all I just described: lashing waves, storms, and the fiercest of winds. No one else survived, so Noah might actually be the one to listen to on this matter of surviving one of the worst, if not the worst time, in history. After all, the Bible records that it was a time when "every intent of the thoughts of [man's] heart was only evil continually," (Genesis 6:5b). At this point in the story, all of our hearts should pound harder and our ears should open wider. We should sit down and listen to how this story unfolds and to anyone who lived through it.

So society was totally corrupt and God had had it! He decided to eradicate mankind from the face of the earth with a great flood. *However*, there was a man found to be righteous in God's eyes: his name was Noah.

God gave Noah a plan to survive the flood and Genesis 7:5 says, "And Noah did according to all that the Lord commanded him." God told Noah exactly how to build a shelter that would save him and his family. Exactly. He gave him blueprints, specific measurements, even what kind of material to use. The ark would serve as God's provision, as His place of safety and protection in perilous times, and finally, as God's instrument of deliverance.

There is no record of rain having ever fallen on the earth before the flood. Noah was about to embark on an unknown journey, a kind of maiden voyage. He was headed into uncharted waters in an untested vessel. Similarly, in marriage a couple is headed into uncharted waters in an untested vessel. While the couple may have loved each other, while they may have been previously married to others or even have lived together, these two people about to wed have never been married to one another before. Therefore, they have not tested the strength of the marriage vessel or their ability to navigate new waters. It is a journey into the unknown. You will find the latest statistics generally concur with these figures: 41% of 1st marriages will end in divorce, 60% of 2nd marriages, and 73% of 3rd marriages end in divorce. (check out www.

divorcestatistics.org). Marriage is as at risk for extinction as many animal groups. And what is the state of marriages that do survive? Of the marriages that remain intact, a large number are barely surviving instead of thriving. Many are drowning in the seas of conflict, unfaithfulness, and self-centeredness.

The very thought of marriage, the concept of two, of a "we," the design of family and community, all originated in the mind of God. Marriage was an idea birthed out of His love for us. The good news is that God has thoroughly equipped us to build the marriage ark to withstand the perilous times in which we live. I agree with David: "Unless the Lord builds the house, they labor in vain who build it," (Psalms 127:1). We would be foolish not to heed God's blueprints for a healthy and thriving marriage. There is a simple principle most of us who grew up in Sunday school were taught very early through a song. The wise man built his house on a rock and when the rains came, the house stood firm. The foolish man built his house on the sand and when the rains came, the house fell. This story comes from Matthew 7:24–27. Hopefully, we don't just think of it as a cute little song but as a principle to live out in our adult life.

Clearing the Land

When Noah was given the instruction to build an ark, one of his first challenges was finding a place to build such a large "house." When a physical house is built, you first must select a site. You must find a firm place, clear the land, haul off rocks and debris, and level the ground. One thing is certain in the parable we referred to regarding building on rock or sand: the rains WILL come, the winds WILL blow, and the marriage ark WILL be tossed about on the sea of life. In order to withstand these storms, the marriage ark must be constructed on cleared ground.

When I think of preparing the ground for marriage—the building site—I find the site is YOU. Yes, you and the heart you bring. You, consisting of body, soul, and spirit. Marriage starts where YOU are. Marriage itself will not make you committed, honest, or pure in heart. Nor will it miraculously transform you into a godly man or woman. It will not deliver you from lust, dishonesty, depression, or your fantasy life. Many marry with hidden agendas of changing a few things (or even a lot of things) in their mates once the vows are taken. Over and over again, this tactic has led to disappointment and despair. So whether you are just starting out, or whether you have already built, you can look again at YOU.

Can you imagine starting to lay the foundation of a physical house on land that has potholes and stones and clumps of weeds on it? The very foundation would not be level and in no time would develop cracks. So the potholes must be found and filled. The rocks must be cleared or disaster will follow. So what are the proverbial holes? I think the holes represent wounds where hurts have been buried, but often buried alive. I call them holes in the soul. These are the losses resulting in fears of abandonment or rejection. They could be deep disappointments such as betrayals, resulting later in guardedness, living in an attempt to control, and even living in some mild depression. Examples of rocks on the land could be temper flares, any kind of addiction, or financial problems resulting in debt.

How would one of these manifest in marriage? Let's say Jen had a form of an addiction. She is hooked on clothes, make-up, shoes, and purses to the point of running up debt or at least spending money Don wishes could go toward the kids' college education. Don is good-hearted, easygoing, and he really loves Jen. After their talks, she promises to do better. Don, in his life, was already set up to be a rescuer because his mother was an alcoholic who was always going to do better. Don has grown up pulling for the underdog to do better. He fails to recognize these are two sides of the same coin. But shortly into the marriage, he happens to run across a receipt for a dress that cost $255. Jen had presented the dress to him the day she bought it as a little something on the sale rack for which she only paid $49. Now what? The addiction didn't stop just because Jen married a man who loved her. Don is now devastated by the lie. Trust is broken. What else has she lied about? He goes ballistic on her. And did I mention, when Don goes ballistic, he sounds exactly like her father, lecturing and preaching to her about the virtues of honesty? They are now off and running. Cracks in the foundation.

Reality Checks

For those not yet married, ask yourself this question: "If I married this person today, just as they are, and they never change one thing, will I still love them?" If the answer is "no," then you either have to sadly walk away or there is significant work to do. Never buy into the lie, "so-and-so will change once we're married." Maybe they will. Maybe they won't. Maybe they'll change in unexpected or undesired ways. Maybe you will change. And while it is fine to talk about your wants and hopes and needs, you must absolutely take the blinders off, face red flags you have seen flying, and address those instincts in your gut. Whatever you see now is the person at their very best. People with a rescue mentality tend to think "All the other person needs is a good man/woman by their side, someone to believe in them." Maybe so. I encourage you to do the work of making things better *before* you take your vows. Also, patterns of arguing have to be taken into account: matters of intensity and duration, how often each person is being triggered, and what periods of shutting down and withdrawal look like.

I have often said, tongue-in-cheek maybe (but sometimes for real), that I would like to see some changes in the traditional American wedding garb. Instead of the perfectly dressed bride in her white gown and the groom in his handsome tuxedo, I would prefer that the groom be carried in on a stretcher all bloodied and bandaged, by his groomsmen. And the bride could be carried on her gurney by the bridesmaids. They could be laid out side-by-side and then the questions could be asked, "Do you, Daniel, take Joan to be your lawfully wedded wife? Do you want to honor and cherish each other, beaten up and broken, and participate in the healing of Joan's wounds?" Then Joan would be challenged with the same questions regarding Daniel. For the truth is, you will each rip and gouge these wounds in daily life, thus deepening them, or you will be a balm and a salve that facilitates the healing of those same wounds.

Why am I picturing these people bloodied and bandaged? Is everyone wounded? Yes, but to different degrees. It is my experience after three decades of working in private practice and sitting with literally thousands of individuals, couples, and families that no one in this culture has gone unscathed. I believe that by age 18, most young adults have already sustained major losses and have already suffered significant betrayals, rejections, and disappointments.

So it is in the taking of vows "for better or worse" that each partner, with their emotional bruises and deep wounds, commits to become united with the other. As they begin to walk life's journey side-by-side, each becomes part of the healing of the other. We will examine the potential impact on a marriage these bruises, wounds, and all the baggage we bring into a marriage may have.

Another reason for reality checks is that as individuals enter into a marriage, their Technicolor ® fantasies regarding their mate and marriage must soon confront reality. Reality, which may not be pretty and rarely lives up to expectations, can quickly produce disillusionments. This may result in "united" becoming "untied." During these developments, actions and decisions by the partners will determine whether the marriage will thrive or die.

If you have spent some years within marriage, I invite you to stop the tape, so to speak, and ask these questions: based on the state of my mate right now, have I contributed to the healing of hurts in the past or have I contributed to opening old wounds wider, or perhaps creating new wounds in their heart? How is the posture of my heart toward their fears, their struggles? Is my heart basically *for* them…or *against* them? How would my mate answer these questions? What steps am I willing to take if I am not satisfied with the answers I am facing?

The Land of Your Hearts

A serious and conscientious survey must be made over the land of your hearts. An honest look at attitudes and sin patterns is needed in order to clear the land. After prayerfully searching, any secrets that have been identified need to be confessed to your partner BEFORE the wedding ceremony. Too many people start building in a field full of sharp boulders, stumbling blocks, shifting sands, and sinkholes. In some cases, they are not able to endure even the usual disagreements that exist in a relationship. Some of the hidden issues I often run into in counseling are past abortions, or having paid for abortions with another relationship, past sexual abuse (both males and females), a past affair with a married man or woman, even a past marriage that is hidden. If you are married already, realize that these secrets take up space in the relationship. In psychology the premise is that secrets weaken relationships.

The other set of issues that constitute boulders are in the realm of addiction. One reason we look so closely at addictive patterns in individuals is that they are so overpowering in relationships. These addictions can quickly become as dangerous as a mistress and cause the mate to compete for time, money, and the heart itself. By all means let's use a zoom lens on this most devastating toxic poison in relationships. The two most common forms of addictions affecting marriage are, of course, alcohol and pornography, and close behind are illegal and over-the-counter drugs, gambling, spending, rage, and food.

The most common misperception by both parties on the subject of pornography is that the problem will all go away once the couple can freely have all the sex they want. Not true. So not true! Either party, male or female, may have had a very promiscuous past. That will affect the intimacy of the relationship, especially if it goes under the radar. Pornography use specifically feeds into a greater ability to compartmentalize one's mind and spirit. Little secret compartments. Dirty white lies can lead to dirty big deceptions. Pornography, like any addiction, demands more and more to feed it and keep it alive. Yes, it does affect the ability to love. Yes, it does affect intimacy. Couples will even try to watch pornography or X-rated movies together as a means to stir up passion. It will be a toxic element introduced into intimacy and the couple will come to depend on it for love and passion to happen.

Overconsumption of alcohol is another huge culprit in a couple's demise. Tom had a habit of going out with the guys one night a week before he and Lynn married. She thought that would slow down once he had her to come home to. Wrong. Just one night a week... right? The habit rocked along until there were sporadic nights that Tom wouldn't show up until 1 or 2 a.m., and an occasional 4 a.m. And in my office, it is rare to hear a story of a knock-down, drag-out fight occurring without alcohol. You may be thinking, "Margaret, it's the 2000's! Loosen up and get with the times!" Well friends, I am very much with the times. I am in the times of a divorce every 13 seconds. So I am here to sniff out the culprits. All full-blown addictions will wreak havoc within a marital relationship. All the books in the world would not hold the stories of heartache and havoc wrought by addictions.

We also need to take a close look at past hurts represented by punctures and cuts and bruises to the heart. This is not to ingrain a victim mentality or to play the blame game, but to be sure the wound has been cleaned out and healed. Dave had two alcoholic parents. They divorced when he was 12 and his mother moved across the country. He was in full-blown identity formation at 12 and ended up in what amounted to a foreign land. He lost his peer group, his father, his home, and basically, his identity. By the time he met his wife-to-be, he appeared to be a grown man, well-adjusted, and responsible. The hole was well covered. But it was not healed. The infection remained in the wound which spilled out in toxic ways whenever a life circumstance would re-open it. Deep periods of depression would occur seemingly out of nowhere. These periods would be lonely stretches of time for his wife who couldn't understand why he could not "be happy." After all, he had the family now he always wanted. The unhealed past invades the present. Things unhealed will work their way to the top just like a splinter.

Mary had been raped in her teenage years. She kept it a secret because of who it was and buried it underneath layers of cement. In her dating life she became very seductive. When her husband dated her, he had no clue of any intimacy issues. Shortly into the marriage she became very busy conveniently at bedtime. Mary and Jesse didn't have a good skill set in the communication department and things deteriorated around this long-held secret.

This is why I ask people to take a long, hard look at their heart-land. Are there holes? Are there rocks? Bitterness, fear, and mistrust can lurk, manifested in the present as control, anger, and defensiveness. Please take time to survey your personal land. Dig deep. Write down the past hurts, disappointments, betrayals, losses, and rejections. Hold each one up and ask God to show you what remains around that hurt. Be honest about addictive patterns. What patterns have been there in the past? What has been present in the past year? Use rigorous honesty, as they suggest in Alcoholics Anonymous. What does it take to do this kind of inventory? It takes courage. It takes tenacity. It demands humility. "Search me, O God, and know my heart. Try me, and know my anxieties," (Psalms 139:23). Also join with David in this request: "Create in me a clean heart, O God, and renew a steadfast spirit within me," (Psalms 51:10). One more thing… this search demands a strong desire to love another, to truly cherish them, to participate in healing and not tearing of their wounds, the desire to have the ability to be faithful. Enter with no secrets. If secrets remain, confess them. Enter as whole as possible. Enter with a clean heart and clean hands. In order to have a sure foundation, the preliminary work is well worth it. If you have entered marriage already and the foundation has cracks, go back to the beginning. His mercies are new every morning.

"Create in me a clean heart, O God, and renew a steadfast spirit within me,"

(Psalms 51:10).

Personal Inventory: Surveying the Land

Rate yourself on a scale of 1 to 10 on the following statements:

My Relationship to God

My relationship to God is
distant
close and intimate

My time in the Word is
nonexistent
mundane
meaningful

My worship time is
going through the motions
alive and inspiring

My life
is a dim light
fully reflects His righteousness

God…
I hardly remember Him
He invades and permeates my everyday life

I hardly think to pray anymore
My prayer life sustains me

My Relationship to Myself

I don't like myself very much
I am comfortable with myself

I have a lot of self-doubt
I am self-confident in most situations

I live with condemnation in my head
I give myself grace

I carry a lot of guilt
I have forgiven myself of my sins and failures

I am critical of others to lift myself
I respect the person I am

I am *immature and reactionary*
I am mature

I am *irresponsible*
I am responsible

My Relationship to Others

I *often break my word*
am a promise keeper

I pay
late or the interest only and keep charging
pay my debts on time

I *hold grudges*
am forgiving in general

I handle disappointments *poorly*
well

I *compromise on truth when it is uncomfortable*
am honest all the time

I *stuff, repress, and withhold my feelings*
express my feelings

I have a *volatile temper*
even temper

I *use profanity often*
have clean speech

I have been sober* *less than 6 months*
at least 6 months

I *am holding on to offenses*
have forgiven my abusers

*sober refers to the absence of addictive behaviors—alcohol, drugs, overspending, or participating in any form of sex outside of marriage including masturbation or pornography.

Conversation Starters

Review your PERSONAL INVENTORY with your partner. Then discuss the following:

1. An area I definitely need to address is…
2. The ways this area affects my life are…
3. The ways this area affects my fiancé / mate are…
4. For me to change, I will need to…
5. If I do not make this change, then…

CHAPTER 2

Held Together by Pitch

Covenants, Vows, and Commitments

"Thus says the Lord: 'If you can break My covenant with the day and My covenant with the night, so that there will not be day and night in their season, then My covenant may also be broken with David My servant,"
(Jeremiah 33:20–21a).

Covenant: *A binding agreement made by two or more; a compact; a contract. A solemn agreement or vow.*

Vow: *An earnest promise or pledge that binds one to perform a specified act or behave in a certain manner.*

Commit: *To place in trust or charge; consign, entrust. To bind or obligate as by a pledge.*

Definitions from the American Heritage Dictionary

God told Noah, "Make yourself an ark of gopherwood; make rooms in the ark, and cover it inside and outside with pitch," (Genesis 6:14). What was the purpose of the pitch, or tar? Was it not to seal the ark and to keep water out which could cause the ark to sink? A commitment is a pledge that binds someone to a course of action. I have heard an illustration regarding commitment that likens it to gluing two pieces of paper together, and then attempting to tear the sheets apart. The two are inseparable, and in trying to tear them apart, you simply rip both pieces. God gives us the opportunity in marriage to learn what commitment to another person really means. He uses marriage to help us mature our character through committing ourselves to the needs of another. In the context of marriage, we are provided with a way to learn about faithfulness and loyalty to another, just as God has committed to us, His bride, and has remained faithful to us throughout our lives.

Mortar and Pestle

When a couple is in love and cannot wait to be together on a daily basis, it is not difficult to face the words "covenants," "vows," and "commitments." Of course, "I promise," but as time unfolds and there are financial struggles, differences rear their heads, and babies may be born, the couple will face the mortar and pestle of relationship.

The marriage is the mortar, the container that holds the couple and their relationship. The pestle is the daily challenge of coming face-to-face with each other's preferences, personalities, and differences. An article on Wikipedia describes the pestle as "a heavy club-shaped object, the end of which is used for crushing and grinding." What a great description! In the bowl of marriage will be revealed our flesh, our triggers, our wounds. Will we be crushed and ground to powder? Or will we be refined into individuals with more tenderness, patience, serving spirits, and greater love? Outcomes of character are forged right here.

Have you heard about a sign posted in some of the jewelry stores in Las Vegas: "We rent wedding rings?" Does that not aptly describe the cynicism, the level of expectation, and the resignation of our times toward the "till death do we part" portion of the marriage ceremony? We are a nation of people plagued by irresponsibility, selfishness, promise-breaking, and rebellion. This pattern of sinfulness is the sociological crucible from which we have emerged. I believe this state of affairs has led to two things: 1) It has led couples to despair and in many cases, decide just to live together and forego the marriage in order to not fail; and 2) It has caused others to dig in their heels, working harder to have a great marriage. Keeping one's word is becoming rarer today, and yet, when promises are kept, such marvelous things happen—bonding occurs, trust is created, hope soars, and relationships are deepened.

Let me take time out to acknowledge this may be a difficult chapter for those who lived through failed marriages and now face taking vows again. All we have the here and now. I invite you to be willing to give a close examination of your heart at this point. Please consider any hurts from the past you feel are unhealed, resentments still held, or anything else that would spill out on another loved one. Be as healthy and whole a person as you know how to be. If you find you need to go through more counseling or healing prayer or whatever else is needed, be willing to take those steps. We all work things out before our God. Inviting Him to continue the healing of our losses, regrets, and wounds is the responsibility we all bear. Also, the work of offering and receiving forgiveness is a necessary element of leaving the past behind and pressing forward. We all should embrace Lamentations 3:22–23: "Through the Lord's mercies we are not consumed, because His compassions fail not. They are new every morning; great is Your faithfulness."

Counting the Cost Before You Build the Tower

Jesus asked, "For which of you, intending to build a tower, does not sit down first and count the cost, whether he has enough to finish it?" (Luke 14:28). I tell those in my premarital classes there is not a way to count the cost of this tower, the one to be built with marriage vows. Commitment always involves risks and unknowns. We have a modern day example in a very public figure, Christopher Reeve and his wife. A tragic accident suddenly left him a quadriplegic. His wife did not know at the time of her vows all that would be required from her in order to keep her promise to "love, honor, and cherish him, in good times and in bad."

Bringing it close to home, when my husband Gary and I married, he was working on a career in physics and I was working towards a career in music. I envisioned us settling down in an upper-middle class neighborhood, raising our children, and I would eventually become president of the PTA while he went to a successful job every day. This is what I signed up for. I had not a clue we would end up living in a fourth-world country in West Africa. I had not even heard of the country, Sierra Leone. No plans were laid to have babies in a little house 5,000 miles from home. I did not know Gary would go through a life-threatening bout of cancer. I did not know he would retool from physics to ministry and I would have a role for 20 years as a minister's wife, not the president of the PTA. You could write a list of your own twists and turns that were quite surprising: the moves, the illnesses, the losses and gains you could not have imagined.

Our personal friends, Marlie and Kiefer, were blindsided by life with his sudden diagnosis of a terminal illness with no possible treatment. The following few months, living with this untenable situation at the age of 30, Marlie certainly felt anything but equipped. She, however, has said it was the hardest journey to go through but the easiest promise to keep. Neither of them could have counted the cost of building the marriage tower.

The glue, the pitch, holding the planks together in these times when individuals are exhausted, disheartened, hurt, and torn, are the promises made, the vows declared. So how we count the cost is knowing we don't know all that will be required, all that it will take. We take the vows in faith that God will supply what we need when we need it.

Sealing the Contract

Commitment is described in scripture through the concept of a covenant. A covenant is a permanent contract. The words "permanent contract" may sound pretty cold-hearted, but God also illuminates the beauty and the heart of a covenant when He makes a covenant with Israel to "love you forever" and then calls them the "apple of His eye," (Deuteronomy 32:10). The word "covenant" is from the Hebrew word "berith" meaning determination, stipulation, covenant, treaty, or pledge. A contract accompanied by signs, sacrifices, and a solemn oath sealed a relationship with promises of blessings for adhering to the contract and with curses for breaking the contract.

I have always found the ancient concept of arranged marriages to be fascinating. "Here is your wife, now learn to love each other." Implied in that is, "choose to love each other." The story of Isaac and Rebekah is stark in my mind. Abraham asks his eldest servant to place his hand under his thigh and take an oath (notice another example of covenant making). The servant was to swear that he would find a wife for Isaac, not among the Canaanites, but from among his own people group. So the servant goes to Nahor and stands by a well and prays. Yes, he doesn't just use his instincts or look for the prettiest woman. He prays for God to help him through a sign. However, when Rebekah appeared, she was indeed very beautiful and she fulfilled the sign in a perfect way, (Genesis 24:12–17). After the servant has delivered Rebekah to Isaac, scripture says, "Isaac brought Rebekah into his mother Sarah's tent; and he took Rebekah and she became his wife, and he loved her." (Genesis 24:67a). How simple is that!

Understanding the heart of God toward covenant is one of the biggest motivators we can gain. As we look at the time of Abram, we see a "contract" unfold in the Old Testament in Genesis 15. God tells Abram to count the stars, and then He makes a promise to Abram: "So shall your descendants be." Then God promised that Abram would inherit the land where he stood. Abram asks, "How shall I know that I will inherit it?" God has Abram bring a three-year-old heifer, a three-year-old female goat, a three-year-old ram, a turtledove, and a young pigeon. He then cut all but the birds in half. A deep sleep comes over Abram in which horror and great darkness fall on him. God spells out his covenant again. In verses 17 and 18 we read, "And it came to pass, when the sun went down and it was dark, that behold, there appeared a smoking oven and a burning torch that passed between those pieces. On the same day the Lord made a covenant with Abram." God's token was the passing of fire between the animal halves sacrificed by Abram and Abram's token to God was circumcision.

Today, we have the exchange of rings as tokens of the marriage covenant. Many meaningful metaphors have been spoken around the exchange of rings, such as the unbroken circles of love they represent. A story that still moves me today is one of a particular woman's recount of the tear she experienced in her heart as she removed that circle from her finger after more than 30 years of marriage ended in divorce.

The Heart of the Covenant

The "contract" made on the wedding day is not just a business deal, signed and sealed. It is not upheld as the law is upheld. It is not a set of rules to simply follow, but it represents a personal relationship in the same way our relationship with God is a personal relationship, not a legalistic one. It is a covenant made by *choosing*. Like Ruth's covenant with Naomi, it will require moving into unfamiliar territory. God continually *chooses* us, over and over again. And in marriage, there is the *choice* to enter the covenant. But beyond that, we must continue on, hour-by-hour, day-by-day, *choosing* our mate.

Our covenant with God today that allows us to be adopted sons and daughters brings great comfort to my own heart. For I know that if God says it, it will be. I know that He will not grow weary of the covenant He has made with me. I know that it is forever and will hold up under the weight of my sins, my failures, and the multitude of my shortcomings because of His faithfulness. Also in Deuteronomy (7:6–8), God speaks of His "forever love" in these terms:

> For you are a holy people to the Lord your God; the Lord your God has chosen you to be a people for Himself, a special treasure above all the peoples on the face of the earth. The Lord did not set His love on you nor choose you because you were more in number than any other people, for you were the least of all peoples; but because the Lord loves you, and because He would keep the oath which He swore to your fathers, the Lord has brought you out with a mighty hand, redeemed you from the house of bondage, from the hand of Pharaoh king of Egypt.

God said in Jeremiah 33:20–21a, "Thus says the Lord: 'If you can break My covenant with the day and My covenant with the night, so that there will not be day and night in their season, then My covenant may also be broken with David My servant." The nature of God is promise-keeping. Jesus is the Son of Promise.

The original covenant of marriage will be kept through hundreds, maybe thousands of daily kept promises. Each time your word is kept, trust is sealed. Pitch allowed certain elements to be kept safe inside and other dangerous elements were kept out. Consider what is kept safe when a promise is kept. I think of things like love, hope, trust, and faith.

The original covenant of marriage will be kept through hundreds, maybe thousands of daily kept promises. Each time your word is kept, trust is sealed. Pitch allowed certain elements to be kept safely inside the ark and other dangerous elements were kept out. Consider what is kept safe when a promise is kept. I think of things like love, hope, trust, and faith.

I often picture marriage like a big fishing net. Each kept promise is like a knot tied in the net. Each broken promise makes a tear in the net. A broken place is called a breach. When a breach occurs in a relationship, distance occurs. Distance plus more distance creates a chasm. Paying attention to one's words in the small and big matters of life makes a huge difference. Whether it's a promise to carry out the trash or be home by 5:30, it is your word that is on the line. Scripture explains that it is "the little foxes that spoil the vines," (Song of Solomon 2:15). So please pause. Take a look at any patterns of lying, patterns of broken promises. Just examine the little foxes that might become bigger and more impacting.

Mutual Love and Respect

Another part of covenant keeping within a marriage is balance. When a marriage is out of balance between the partners, it can look like a see-saw. One has power, the other none. Or one is acting parental, the other childish. One is subservient, the other dominant. While we each have roles and unique personalities, those roles and personalities should complement and bring balance to our spouse. "Like a seesaw, it is the under functioning of one individual that allows for the over functioning of the other," (Lerner, 1985). This can give the feeling of a parent-child relationship instead of partners facing the world as a united and singular front. For example, if a man feels nagged by his wife, he may respond by being noncompliant to her requests. The less he responds to her, the less she feels heard. The less heard and valued and acknowledged she feels, the more she nags and demeans him. The less respected he feels, the more he ignores her. And thus, the balance of a marriage has sunk into stereotypes of bullying and nagging.

Our marriage covenant is similar to the covenant between God and Israel. In light of the constant breaking of marriage covenants in our day through affairs, our culture is definitely reenacting God's forever love and Israel's covenant-breaking. It is such a gift that we have the opportunity, by receiving this kind of love from God, to love one another in the same way. Our covenant is a binding agreement recognized by God and the laws of the land. This arrangement is permanent: "I will betroth you to Me forever," (Hosea 2:19a). Obviously, it takes the commitment of *two* to keep the covenant. Only by His strength and upholding arm can we be covenant-makers and covenant-keepers!

> "*Therefore know that the Lord your God, He is God, the faithful God who keeps covenant and mercy for a thousand generations with those who love Him and keep His commandments,*"
>
> (Deuteronomy 7:9).

Conversation Starters

1. Discuss with your partner examples of times when you have not kept your word.
2. Discuss excuses and rationalizations you find yourselves using in your own mind or to your partner when you have broken your word. (For example: the wife agrees on a grocery budget but sees a great buy at the store, one she cannot pass up because it will save money later. What would be her guiding principle here? What are the rationalizations? What would the eventual repercussions be if this happened in many "little" instances?)
3. Discuss how trust is broken when your mate doesn't keep his or her word. (Examples: not being on time, overspending, procrastinating in chores, neglecting to get the car fixed.)

4. How can you keep your word at all times? Answer: By staying in agreement. You may renegotiate a previous agreement and then you can live within the parameters of the new negotiation.

CHAPTER 3

The Building Tools

"And do not be conformed to this world, but be transformed by the renewing of your mind, that you may prove what is that good and acceptable and perfect will of God,"
(Romans 12:2).

The Building Tools

Whether Noah developed sophisticated tools or worked with rather crude tools, we do not know. We do know, however, that he had to clear the land, chop down trees, split the wood, put the planks together, frame the inside rooms, and do other such tasks. There had to be a standard of measurement because God had given instructions in specifics. I believe life and death hung in the balance for Noah and his family. And I believe Noah took God's instructions seriously. I think he referred often to the blueprints, for he not only had an obedient heart, but his life and the life of his family depended on the safety of the ark. Noah had to listen carefully, have an "ear to hear," and believe that God knew more than he did. This posture indicates a contrite heart (acknowledging his own limitations). Noah had to follow his hearing by doing. What an awesome task God had laid out for him!

Almost every facet of life changes to some degree when a couple marries. Now they must learn to think, feel, and act as a couple rather than as individuals. They must give up unilateral decision making for mutuality. Living as husband and wife means sacrificing some independence and personal desires for the benefit of this living, breathing entity we call *marriage*. When we begin to build our marriages and attempt to live out the principles of love, respect, and forgiveness, more of our fleshly nature will be revealed than ever before. We will discover that some of our tools are misshapen, bent, and some are missing altogether. If the tools we are using are bent and out of shape, then the ark of marriage we build may not be a very safe place – ill-prepared to endure the storm-tossed sea of life.

Shaping a World View in the Family Crucible

The original crucible for the shaping of our lives is the family in which we grow up. It is here we learn our first tools for relationships. Later in life, school, church, peer groups, and many other influences become part of the shaping. Without a doubt the family experience has the greatest influence. Sociologists use the term *family of origin* to describe the family into which we are born and grow up, the crucible in which we develop our view of others, the world, God, and ourselves. Here, our attitudes, value systems, rituals, likes and dislikes are formed. Each family has its own encoded language and labels for what is good or bad, nice or ugly, valuable or worthless. Attached to these labels are values or "price tags" which then become associated with every conceivable object: from the President of the United States to the Pope; from broccoli and soybeans to ribeye steaks; and from the value of your parakeet to the value of your grandmother.

There are families whose soil-environment readily provides nutrients of love, honesty, and forthright communication, where principles of honor and respect are modeled in consistent ways. In these homes, there is not only teaching, but also the living out of forgiveness, self-sacrifice, and promise-making as well as promise-keeping. There are families at the other extreme of the spectrum, modeling unforgiveness, anger, rage, promise-breaking, name-calling, and shame-based relationships. In between, there are families who hit and miss on all these issues, doing better at time than at others. No one has ever done it perfectly, for we are all humankind. The important thing is to identify and be aware of tools that do not work, because their use will cause leaks in your boat!

Juan's father grew up in Mexico and came to America as a young man, already divorced, leaving behind a son he wouldn't see for many years. He met Juan's mother, who already had a baby and an ex-husband. Together, they had Juan and another daughter. Juan grew up in a very violent and volatile home, seeing his mom get hit, as well as being beaten by his father regularly. Juan saw substance abuse in his father as well. His parents divorced when he was young and his father passed away a few years later, while he was still in his teens. The divorce and the death of his father substantially shaped him. Juan had to work from a very young age to contribute financially to his impoverished family. When he moved out on his own, he decided that what he saw growing up was not what he wanted for himself. He took what he saw, what he experienced, and crafted what he wanted: a peaceful home filled with love and respect. He decided to try and live differently.

Juan grew up surrounded with broken and bent and misshapen tools for relationships. The ark in his family was never functional, never a protective place. But his story is not unique. Many of us grew up in less than ideal circumstances with boats that could not float because the tools were not well-crafted. But we can choose different tools and create a new ark for ourselves as adults. While our family of origin shapes us greatly, it does not have to define our choices and our future and our marriage ark.

Jane grew up in an unsafe atmosphere. When her parents fought, it was loud, and at times she could hear the breaking of glass or the car screeching out of the driveway. She became very quiet, very seldom letting her true feelings out. And she definitely stayed on the fringes, lest she become a target. When she married Rusty, she brought with her the tool kit she had forged in her first intimate relationships, those of her family of origin. They worked as ways to protect herself then. Now she was in a totally different environment. Rusty was open, spontaneous, and playful. When Jane got quiet and went into retreat mode, he was baffled and tried to get her to talk, to share what was going on. She found this annoying and often would say, "Why can't you just leave me alone? That's just the way I am." This game of hide-and-seek got old very quickly. The very tools that worked so well back in the family felt like a shield she could hide behind. But Rusty played tug-of-war with the shield, leaving her vulnerable. The bottom line was this tool did not work in her present situation. It kept her from intimacy, vulnerability, and sharing with the heart of her husband.

Distilling the Issues

Marriage is filled with "issues." We hear a lot about "*processing the issues*." We hope that couples reach resolve on the majority of their issues early on, because if they don't, these will remain as stones in their shoes. Let's consider some of the major issues in marriage. The obvious ones are finances, religious beliefs and practices, sex, how time is spent, communication, raising of children, and relationships with in-laws and extended families. Outlying issues may be things like division of labor, hobbies, food preferences, expressions of affection, friend preferences, and other similar issues. We can expand this list exponentially if we think of the myriad of details included in everyday life.

There are an infinite number of issues that will emerge with each developmental stage in a couple's life. The challenge is going to remain in *how* these issues will be distilled. How will the couple boil all the facets down into one agreed upon answer? I believe couples will always have issues to be addressed, but the real challenge is *how* they will be addressed. Will we teach, bargain, demand, negotiate, pull rank, or play points that have be saved, to name a few? Central to all of this is, what will be the stance of heart, the posture of the heart, in dealing with the item on the table? Will it be a basic "I want what I want"? What happens if both people in the coupleship take this approach? And what if they want different things?

Joe always pictured having some land, living out of the city, raising children where they could run, roam, and climb trees. This felt idyllic to him. Joe was married to Kris and her ideal setting was living in a subdivision with neighbors close by. She pictured her children running into the neighbors' yards and playing in groups, her being able to walk across the street to a friend's for morning coffee. What tools do Joe and Kris need to problem solve this big issue? This issue, by the way, was a very important stalemate that was brought into my office. This and hundreds of other issues will demand skillful tools to navigate these waters that can potentially sink the marriage ark.

In Joe's family of origin when a big issue appeared, his father would state loudly what he wanted, slam a door, and screech out of the driveway. His mom would go to the bedroom, cry, and cook dad a really nice supper when he returned. Needless to say, Joe was unequipped to handle big and sometimes, small, problems that demanded healthy ways to negotiate.

What does all this have to do with a stance of heart? Pretty much everything. It will demand high levels of love, capacity to listen, ability to trust, degrees of self-worth, well-developed maturity—definitely a full tool belt!

The manner in which you responded to your circumstances growing up, whatever they were, will determine the formation of your unique style of problem-solving for building the marriage relationship. Your patterns of process and response will be well-engrained by the time you say, "I do." Hopefully, you will be able to identify such negative traits and attitudes as tendencies to blame, a quick temper, or a desire to shut down and avoid. After becoming aware of these dents in your jar of clay, you can take these things to the Potter and ask for His help in reshaping more godly attitudes. Certainly, there are positive traits and attitudes that will serve to build up, just as there are negative traits and attitudes that tear down.

No worthy purpose is served in dissecting our families of origin in order to excuse us. In other words, seeing our families as causative agents will only go so far, because at some point, we become responsible to God for our own actions. I believe there is value, however, in identifying specific patterns that have developed into strongholds in one's own life.

Technology has developed modern weapons of war, like a bomb that can be dropped miles from its destination and directly hit its target. Likewise, by identifying specific negative strongholds, our divine weapons can be launched with great accuracy to tear them down.

The Developmental Tasks of Marriage

God did not merely tell Noah, "build an ark, save yourself, your family, and all animals. I am about to destroy the world." Instead,

God gave Noah a very specific blueprint with dimensions and materials to use. Like the ark, God has given us a blueprint for marriage. He delivers it beautifully when He said through Paul, "Husbands, love your wives, just as Christ also loved the church…husbands ought to love their own wives as their own bodies," (Ephesians 5:25, 28a). Verse 29 goes on to say, "For no one ever hated his own flesh, but nourishes and cherishes it, just as the Lord does the church." Perhaps you, as a man, were not the recipient of nourishment. Now it is your task to nurture. What does this look like? What does this feel like? How do you know how to do it if you have not seen it? How do you forge a tool or a set of tools to nourish?

Blueprints are important, without a doubt. But blueprints without execution are useless. To execute a plan, we must have the necessary tools. The tools must function, not be bent, broken, or otherwise distorted. We may enter a marriage with some tools that are easily accessible and fully functional. We may start out missing some critical tools. However, the tools in our toolbox will constantly change. Tools break and become outdated. Each phase of life requires a unique set of tools. Truth be told, during the course of a marriage, you will be married to many different people. Choose to love them all! Develop the tools needed at each phase to love one another well. A twenty-five-year-old woman does not have the same communication needs, personality, desires, goals, etc. as a fifty-year-old or an eighty-year-old. That's a good thing. Nor is a thirty-year-old man the same person he will be at seventy-five. A parent is not the same as an empty-nester or a grandparent. You will both change. Choose to change together. Choose to know one another at every phase. Choose to keep your toolbox updated to match you and your spouse's stage of life.

Tools such as honesty, vulnerability, managing resources, being a clear communicator, handling disappointments, learning self-discipline, and resolving conflict are universal tools needed to navigate the waters of life in a functional way at the least, and a joyful and peaceful life at the most.

Life's changing seasons and circumstances will require that we master certain developmental tasks. Marriage brings many challenges: separating from the family of origin, working out mutually negotiated rules for living and loving, establishing communication patterns that nurture the relationship, learning to problem solve, developing strategies that lead to emotional, spiritual, and physical intimacy, and managing money and other resources. It is perhaps a lifelong challenge to leave "me" and become a "we." A couple will depend on the tools in their toolbox to learn the skills to work out the tasks inherent in their marriage.

This instruction, husbands love your wives and wives respect your husbands, from God identifies the challenge of transformation into Christ-likeness that lies before us all. We all need heart transplants REPEATEDLY! Ezekiel, as God's spokesman, told the people, "I will give you a new heart and put a new spirit within you; I will take the heart of stone out of your flesh and give you a heart of flesh," (Ezekiel 36:26). This was not spoken only to "adult children" of alcoholics or only to people who grew up in other dysfunctional families, but to all of God's people – His precious children in Ezekiel's day as well as in our own. Paul admonishes us: "...let us cleanse ourselves from all filthiness of the flesh and spirit, perfecting holiness in the fear of God," (2 Corinthians 7:1).

Let's take a hopeful attitude towards developing our tools. All it takes is a student-heart, a willingness to learn, and some diligent practice.

> *"I will give you a new heart and put a new spirit within you; I will take the heart of stone out of your flesh and give you a heart of flesh,"*
>
> (Ezekiel 36:26).

Conversation Starters

1. Three faulty/destructive tools I am bringing (or have brought) into our relationship are:

2. Choose one of the above to describe to your fiancé (or mate) and then complete the sentence: "The way I have used this tool in the past is…" (See if you can find the purpose of the tool here. Example: withdrawal can be used to punish and get back at your mate, to protect yourself, to feel better than the other person, or to feel in control.)

3. God has my life on the anvil and is changing _____ into _____. (Romans 12:2 "And do not be conformed to this world, but be transformed by the renewing of your mind, that you may prove what is that good and acceptable and perfect will of God.")

4. What I receive when I use the new, improved tools is:

CHAPTER 4

Communication I
Nuts and Bolts

"For if the trumpet makes an uncertain sound, who will prepare for battle? So likewise you, unless you utter by the tongue words easy to understand, how will it be known what is spoken?"

(1 Corinthians 14:8–9a).

Communication I: Nuts and Bolts

A gain and again I am convicted by the heart of this man called Noah. As I have said before, his very life and the life of his family were at stake. Everything hinged on the building of this huge floating house. Noah had never seen rain, so he obviously had an established faith in the God who was speaking to him in terms of a coming flood. **Noah listened to God.** Had he not listened and been able to engage in the needed processes of hearing, clarifying, understanding, and working through the "nuts and bolts" of actually building the ark, Noah and his family would have perished. Had Noah and his wife and sons not been able to communicate, there would have been disaster. It was Noah's responsibility to take this message and communicate it to his family.

"Dialogue is to love what blood is to the body. When the flow of blood stops, the body dies. When dialogue stops, love dies and resentment and hate are born. But dialogue can restore a dead relationship." (Howe, 1963). One of my favorite ways to visualize dialogue is to think of it as a bridge over which two people can cross. When communication stops, the bridge is out. Sometimes it must be rebuilt one plank at a time. Dialogue is definitely the lifeblood of a relationship and the "body" will die without it.

Most couples have communication of some kind. But many times it is garbled or unclear, and thus is misunderstood. Each person enters the relationship with his/her own coded language, almost as though one spoke German and the other Italian. Additionally, there are the nuances of body language and intonations of laughter and voice tone. Sound like work? It is! If you have ever learned a foreign language, you will have some idea of how much work it really requires. In actuality, the couple is forging out a third language, one that will belong to them alone. No one else outside the two of them will ever quite understand all the nuances of the language, whether spoken or unspoken. It is quite mystic and romantic, to say the least, and well worth the working out.

God does not want us to flounder in our walk. He desires for His children to flourish. He did not leave us to figure out for ourselves by trial and error what works and what does not. He has equipped us well with principles and guidelines in the area of communication. All we need is a humble heart to learn.

The Power of the Spoken Word

First, we see the *power of speech* and language. In the story of the building of the tower of Babel ("babel" is Hebrew for "confused"), the Lord said, "Indeed, the people are one and they all have one language, and this is what they begin to do; now nothing that they propose to do will be withheld from them," (Genesis 11:6). This is quite a statement. God is commenting on the power of unity here. He says if they acted as "one," speaking the same language, then it would not be possible to stop them. Please let this concept soak in by reading Genesis 11:6 repeatedly. God then proceeds to confuse their language to stop them from building a tower "whose top is in the heavens."

In the New Testament, James compares the power of the tongue to that of a small spark capable of setting a whole forest on fire, (James 3:5). In the counseling arena, I see this concept lived out over and over again. Words thrown out quickly and lightly can set the whole relationship on fire. Proverbs reminds us of the power of words in the direction of goodness and healing: "A word fitly spoken is like apples of gold in settings of silver," (Proverbs 25:11). Consider the power of Jesus' words as they impacted the woman caught in adultery who was brought to Him. His grace-filled heart was revealed in the words, "He who is without sin among you, let him throw a stone at her first," (John 8:7b).

I witness and hear about so much carelessness with words. I hear many all-or-nothing, black-and-white statements. A husband tries to express his dissatisfaction about his wife's housekeeping skills. She retorts back, "I can't please you! I will never do anything good enough for you! Why don't you just go back to your mother and let her do all your laundry and cook and clean for you?" There's the one, two, three punch. The usual result of this kind of retort, possibly followed by tears, would be closing down any possibility of problem solving. This kind of irrational communication would result in no change. No change results in no hope.

If minor things like chores, housekeeping, where will we eat out, etc., cannot be negotiated, how will couples even begin to navigate weighty subjects like sex, finances, discipline of children, care of elderly parents, and other real life situations. So, let's replay the tape using a clean, productive model. John, in a sincere voice, approaches Jennifer with, "Honey, I know your plate is full and you work hard for our family. Our bedroom, however, is a disaster and the piles of laundry are driving me crazy. Could we pick a night this week and dive into it together and get it back in order? I realize I helped create the tsunami."

Yes, our words are powerful. I hear everything from mild miscommunications to outright attacks, spewing adjectives (You are so stupid/useless/ugly/incompetent) all the way to name-calling (You are a worthless piece of garbage who is basically unlovable). Some people never recover from these wounds, for the words cut too deeply and kill the soul. If you have engaged in these vicious attacks, then you have practiced verbal abuse. One of the most traumatizing forms of verbal abuse is the exploitation of the victim in order for the perpetrator to gain a temporary sense of power (Ketterman, 1992).

In the same way, our positive words that express love and care are also powerful: "I love you;" "You are important to me;" "Thank you for being by my side." These words, when supported by actions, constitute emotional bypass surgery. They go past the logic of our minds and enter straight into the recesses of our hearts. So our words have the power to both cut and pierce a heart or to mend and heal a heart. The third chapter in the book of James speaks clearly to the power of words: "Look also at ships: although they are so large and driven by fierce winds, they are turned by a very small rudder wherever the pilot desires. Even so, the tongue is a little member and boasts great things," (James 3:4–5). So may we weigh our words carefully, considering their impact before they leave our mouths.

Hearing with Your Heart

Next, we see the ***power of listening***. It is a very revealing study to go through scripture and note how many times God encouraged His people to *listen*. Many times, He says to *listen carefully*. David spoke God's heart on this subject in one of the Psalms: "But My people would not heed My voice, and Israel would have none of Me. So I gave them over to their own stubborn hearts, to walk in their own counsels. Oh that My people would listen to Me," (Psalms 81:11–13a).

David goes on to say that God would have "fed them also with the finest of wheat and with honey from the rock I would have satisfied you," (Psalms 81:16). We will never know all that we have missed out on because we did not listen. When your beloved is trying to tell you something, so much is at stake! Did you notice in the early part of the passage how *not listening* was connected to a stubborn heart?

Many marriage manuals urge something called *empathic listening*. This kind of listening involves solely a desire to understand what your partner is really saying, what they are really feeling. It has no goal of judging, finding what's wrong with their viewpoint, or finding holes in their logic. It is being fully focused and fully present with an attempt to come to an understanding. One definition I have always liked concerning good communication is "intent equals impact" (Gottman, 1994). In other words, good communication happens only when the listener actually receives what the speaker actually intends to convey.

Not every conversation calls for empathic listening, but every conversation calls for listening. A lot of couple's communications are about coming into agreement about chores and schedules and the everyday stuff of life. The deeper questions of the relationship, specifically the "Do you care?"

questions, are where the exchanges of information happen, contracts are negotiated and established, and deeper matters of the hearts are shared.

Barriers to listening can be distractions, lack of focus and hurriedness. But most important is the condition of the heart. Deeper matters require an ear with the ability to hear what is said and what is not said. It is like tuning your radio dial to the exact spot where the station comes in most clearly. Listening is such a major tool in the relationship kit. Listening speaks volumes. Listening shouts our value of one another; it shouts our care, love, and our affirmation. Listening with the intent to understand is a healing balm, sowing seeds that will produce the fruit of healed relationships, harmony, trust, and ultimately greater intimacy.

The Impact of Distinction

Third, let us note the **power of clarity**. There is a very interesting concept on the power of clear communication right in the middle of Paul's discussion on spiritual gifts. He says, "Even things without life, whether flute or harp, when they make a sound, unless they make a distinction in the sounds, how will it be known what is piped or played? For if the trumpet makes an uncertain sound, who will prepare for battle? So likewise you, unless you utter by the tongue words easy to understand, how will it be known what is spoken?" (1 Corinthians 14:7–9a). I hope it is not too big a leap to pull out this passage from its context on speaking in tongues. I think it perfectly applies. Indistinct sounds can be given through hinting, innuendo, sarcasm, assuming, and mind reading, to name a few. Pause and reflect on this list. Which of these have you used? And which ones do you habitually use to try to get what you want? Paul says a few verses later, "Therefore, if I do not know the meaning of the language, I shall be a foreigner to him who speaks, and he who speaks will be a foreigner to me," (1 Corinthians 14:11). How true it is! Sometimes it takes patience and perseverance to keep on keeping on until the understanding happens, but then no breach is left and unity is preserved.

I would like to emphasize the need for speaking our needs clearly; to just straight-up ask directly for what you want. To do that, you have to identify what that is, of course. But the hinting, hoping, wishing kinds of communication rarely result in what is wanted. Indirect forms of communication include sarcasm, put-downs, whining, complaining and hinting. All these fall in the category of a passive-aggressive style of communication. Many people have never practiced directly asking for what they want and need. Be clear. Set up your partner to win. Paint the bull's-eye on the target. This does not mean you will automatically get what you want. Your mate is not a candy dispenser. However, it significantly increases your chances. And to the mate who answers in the negative, who might say, "No, I can't do that," or "No, I'm not willing to do that," I have established a rule for those clients. The rule says, "Never say no without a yes." So Jim might say, "You know what, honey, I can't get that door painted this week, but I will have it done by the end of next week." This shows a spirit of cooperation and a desire to meet needs. After all, "Hope deferred makes the heart sick," (Proverbs 13:12a).

The Rewards of Patience

Last, I would like to highlight the ***power of waiting***. Quickness is valued highly in our day. I once heard it said in the old days that if a person missed a stagecoach coming through town, they would just catch the next one three months later. But now people get upset if they miss a turn in a revolving door. In the context of Biblical principles of communication, here is an instance where we find *slow is good*. James, who had much to say on this subject, says, "So then, my beloved brethren, let every man be swift to hear, slow to speak, slow to wrath.," (James 1:19). We will look later at the *slow to become angry* aspect, but for now the invaluable lesson is the *slow to speak* concept. James says further in the chapter to keep "a tight rein on our tongue." Now there is a word picture of which to be proud! Maybe this scripture is telling us to spend our time with a greater proportion in listening and a lesser proportion spent in speaking. Only with the reins of the Holy Spirit could this be possible for most of us.

When a couple is dealing with deeper issues, these may demand many conversations, not just one. Some people start one of these at 10 PM and feel compelled to "finish" it before the night is over. They keep going until 3 AM instead of learning to table an issue and have several discussions. When one partner has to be at work at 7:30 AM the next morning and is begging to stop, please learn to wait. Learn to deal with the lack of closure. That is a mark of maturity.

Another part of waiting is being aware of timing on presenting an issue. Generally, it is not a good idea to drop a big problem on your mate as they are hurriedly walking out the door for a meeting, calling them at work in the middle of a busy work day, starting problem solving conversations at bedtime or texting while out of town. Learn to set up meeting times for these heavier conversations.

Reactivity may pay off if a child is running into a busy road, but it rarely pays off in building relationships. Being slow to answer really ties back into areas already touched on: showing value to the person I am trying to understand, putting aside quick judgments, and conveying caring for your mate. For sure, our highest priority in the area of communicating is hearing God and listening to His clear message. Secondly, it is making the investment into our marriage and honoring our mate by listening, clarifying, and being sure we have received the message before we speak. It is the lifeblood of the relationship!

"A word fitly spoken is like apples of gold in settings of silver,"

(Proverbs 25:11).

Conversation Starters

1. If you were going to write a book about your personal style of communicating, what would the title be?

2. From the four traits talked about in this lesson (the spoken word, listening, clarity, and patience), rate yours from strongest to weakest.

3. When you are communicating with your fiancé / mate, what do you want most from them?

4. Name a specific change in your communication that would bring your relationship to a more intimate level.

CHAPTER 5

Communication II
Conflict in the Ark

"Catch us the foxes, the little foxes that spoil the vines, for our vines have tender grapes,"
(Song of Solomon 2:15).

Communication II: Conflict in the Ark

More than likely, spending all that time with people and animals cooped up in the ark must have had its challenges. And to add to all the practical challenges, there must have been relationship challenges. Remember, the people in that boat were all family. I wonder how they negotiated chores such as whose turn it was to feed elephants, calm the monkeys, clean the gerbil cages, prepare the meals, and keep the candlewicks trimmed. Surely, many tests of patience, problem-solving abilities, and the need for creativity must have arisen on a daily if not hourly basis. But somehow I cannot imagine them yelling, screaming, and calling each other names in the midst of the potential chaos. In the big picture, their lives had been spared. They were part of God's big plan for the future. They had a sense of destiny. They were living in God's provision, literally: the ark.

Could not all these things be said of us today? Have not *our* lives been spared? Are *we* not part of God's big plan? Do *we* not have a destiny and are *we* not living in God's literal provision? I wonder how we so quickly lose sight of these amazing truths. What are we so focused on when arguments ensue?

I believe, for the great majority of couples who stand before God and their friends and families, there is every intention of loving and cherishing the person whose hands they are holding. How could it possibly be that, at some future time, things could unravel to the point of cursing and name-calling directed at the one whom they loved so much?

For some answers, I first want to look at the big picture, which is like taking an aerial view across the terrain of marriage. This overview is typically broken down into stages that are commonly recognized by relationship experts. Each stage of marriage presents certain challenges that will determine the level of conflict.

The Challenge of Change

The first stage of a romantic relationship is the ***romanticized*** stage. Preoccupation and even obsessive thinking toward the lover characterize this stage. Each partner sees the other through an optimistic filter, or rose-colored glasses. Thoughts range from playing the record over and over of the last meeting, planning and anticipating the next meeting, overlooking faults, minimizing shortcomings, and focusing on positive traits. Behaviors include extensive dialogue, feedback, laughter, and a great desire for touching and physical contact. The challenge here is to be realistic and to not sweep issues under the rug.

The second stage, which begins after the vows are said, I call the ***realistic*** stage. The thought-life shifts now to dealing with everyday life: the bills that have to be paid, groceries that must be planned and purchased, repairs that have to be made on the house and cars, and so forth. The attention now is more divided as pressures come to bear on the couple. Another critical shift takes place as the filter that blocked out and minimized faults begins to adjust to see the realism of the shortcomings. Behaviorally, there is less time to "attend" to the other person as outside pressures come to the forefront.

This may sound very discouraging to some, but it is without a doubt inevitable. How a couple handles this, I call the ***critical points of choice***. These developments will always present a fork in the road and decisions made here can set the entire future tone for a marriage. It is the choice at this fork that will determine stage three.

If one set of choices is made, stage three will be characterized by ***deeper disappointment and disillusionment***. The thought-life will be dominated by negative thinking: "This person does not understand me," or "He/she does not really care about me." The filter now takes a major shift, now filtering out the positive traits and filtering in the deficits. Feelings are marked by frustration and hopelessness. Behaviorally, there is less dialogue and more arguing and silence. If things continue to unravel, there will be heightened defensiveness. Each will cover their wounds; unilateral decisions will begin to be made rather than the mutual ones, as in the beginning. Later on, some lying will take place in order to avoid conflict. This is extremely treacherous territory, for it is here that the fabric of trust is torn.

If this downward spiral continues, disruptive patterns will emerge, only to play out over and over again. The filter that once filtered in positive traits will most often turn. Now it will literally log and note more negative traits. The language will become more evaluative, using negative adjectives such as, "John is so stubborn, so selfish, so..." Now John will be labeled and put in a box and may have a hard time escaping. The language will become all-or-nothing. "John never comes through," "He never thinks about anyone but himself," and so on. Notice how a deeper hole is dug. Instead of choosing responses, the couple begins reacting with rote comebacks.

But if, at that critical junction, other choices are made, the picture can be one of a ***lifetime of companionship and partnering*** which invites a deepening of the love that was there in the beginning. Moses told the people of God's plan and destiny like this: "...God is bringing you into a good land, a land of brooks of water, of fountains and springs, that flow out of valleys and hills; a land of wheat and barley, of vines and fig trees and pomegranates, a land of olive oil and honey," (Deuteronomy 8: 7–8). This can be your inheritance in the marriage. The thought life will be something like this: "Even if you're not perfect, I still love you and accept you." Realistic expectations come into being. The filter takes both positives and negatives, but is weighted toward the positives. In behavioral terms, decision-making is characterized by mutuality. Open dialogue continues as before marriage. An attitude of respect and honor is communicated through word, body language, and deeds. An environment of hopefulness ("we can find solutions"), affirmation, and encouragement is present. In many ways, the Israelites as mentioned above came to that place of critical choice. It is a sad study to follow the stages I have just talked about in regard to the love relationship between Israel and the God of heaven. Their saga, in a nutshell, began with trust and dialogue and hearts open to God. Through their own *critical points of choice*, their relationship with God deteriorated to the extent that God finally gave Israel a certificate of divorce, (Jeremiah 3:8). However, God, in His precious faithfulness, took back Israel time after time, (Hosea).

In fact, if you will incorporate this idea of *critical points of choice* into everyday life with your partner, it can save you a lot of grief. I remember one time back in early marriage when I was so mad at Gary (for what, I have no idea). It was the one time that I went so far as to get a blanket and pillow and plant myself on the couch. I remember about 5 minutes into this exercise, the thought hit me, "Where is this going to lead?" I am not going to start sleeping on the couch as a way of living, so why am I doing this?" The thought was so stark that it wasn't long at all until I gathered up my pillow and went quietly back to our marriage bed. I never did that again. These points come to us daily in some form or another.

Little Foxes Spoil the Vine

Wisdom stated, "The little foxes spoil the vines, for our vines have tender grapes." What more tender fruit can there be than that which is produced on the marriage vine? Drive out the little foxes. Many things could constitute little foxes and certainly there might be big foxes, too! Some foxes look like selfishness, competitiveness, insecurities, tendencies to keep score, and "little" broken promises. Bigger foxes, sometimes wolves might look like lies, all sorts of addictions, especially pornography in all its forms, alcohol, or drugs.

In the Old Testament, we find the story of Nehemiah who was the cup bearer to the king. He was tremendously burdened over the fallen walls around the city of Jerusalem. The gates had been burned and the city was open prey. Nehemiah received permission to head the task of rebuilding the walls. Just as naysayers taunted Noah as he built a big boat in a time of no rain, naysayers taunted Nehemiah's workers as they rebuilt the wall. It is interesting that one of the taunts made against those who rebuild contains a reference to foxes. Tobiah said, "Whatever they build, if even a fox goes up on it, he will break down their stone wall," (Nehemiah 4:3). But the people had a mind to work, (verse 6b). As Tobiah and others heard that "the gaps were beginning to be closed," (verse 7), they plotted even harder. "Nevertheless we made our prayer to our God, and because of them we set a watch against them day and night," (verse 9).

I believe in Nehemiah is revealed a strategy against the foxes. A wall was built so that the gaps were closed and a guard was posted on the wall. You have probably heard of watchmen on the walls. I think if walls and perimeters are set up around conflict, then the resentments, scorekeeping, and places of unforgiveness can be kept out.

In Dr. John Gottman's famous research study, *Why Marriages Succeed or Fail: And How You Can Make Yours Last*, he describes the specific identifiable stages of the negative spiral (1994). By keeping a "watchman on the wall" one or both partners can recognize these stages and sound the alarm. Gottman compares these to recognizing the known signs of an impending heart attack: i.e. chest pains, numbness in the arm, neck, jaw, shortness of breath, etc. The signs that a marriage is unraveling are basically descriptions of interacting in destructive ways. The first is *criticism*. Here Dr. Gottman is referring to attacking the other and includes the labeling, "You are…" (fill in the blank with negative adjectives). The second stage is *contempt*, which Gottman describes as the intention to insult and psychologically abuse your partner. It includes mocking, sarcasm, insults, and even certain body language. The third spiral is *defensiveness*. If one is hurling insults, it stands to reason that the other partner will become defensive: "Who are you to call me selfish? Who sat on the couch yesterday while I mowed the yard?" And the fourth spiral is *stonewalling*. Now we can literally see the hardened heart. It is as if there is so much defeat, so much hopelessness, and so little energy that there is no reason to talk anymore, no need to try. The silence can be the last insurmountable wall.

I believe the walls of protection are given to us in 1 Corinthians 13, often referred to as the "love chapter." If these guidelines are followed, the gaps will be closed. If there is watchfulness, day and night, to keep these principles, the marriage terrain will remain unspoiled.

I recommend that each of these principles from 1 Corinthians 13 becomes like a brick in the wall, the wall that keeps the foxes out. The *bricks* are made of love. The bricks are labeled like this:

> Love suffers long and is kind; love does not envy; love does not parade itself, is not puffed up, does not behave rudely, does not seek its own, is not provoked, thinks no evil, does not rejoice in iniquity, but rejoices in the truth, bears all things, believes all things, hopes all things, endures all things. Love never fails, (1 Corinthians 13:4–8a).

Read these words often. Assess yourself often. Be honest. Put your name in the place of "love" and as you read "John is patient. John is kind," stop and check your heart. Be the watchman on the wall.

The tender vine of marriage is growing inside these walls. The vine is both amazingly durable and amazingly fragile, because the vine is relationship. The relationship is a three-fold cord, not easily broken. But when it is sliced with accusations, constant criticism, stony silence, name-calling, and threats, the three-fold cord can be cut. In careful prayer and concern, guard the tender vine. Tend it with love and a watchful eye. Then it will flourish and bear fruit for all around. It will provide strength and shade of protection for the whole family when it is full-grown.

> "...if we love one another, God abides in us, and His love has been perfected in us,"
>
> (1 John 4:12b).

Conversation Starters

1. The blueprint for resolving conflict that I grew up with was...

2. When I get to the **critical points of choice** in everyday situations, right now I find myself choosing...

3. Think of a time in your life when the walls were down and the "foxes" got in to "spoil the vine." Where was the watchman, the guard?

4. According to the passage in 1 Corinthians 13, what brick in the wall do you find missing or in critical need of repair as you relate to your partner?

5. If you do not find this brick and repair the wall, what "foxes" will likely find their way into your relationship?

CHAPTER 6

Love Boat 101

"And now abide faith, hope, love, these three; but the greatest of these is love,"
(1 Corinthians 13:13).

Love Boat 101

I love to write. I love to try my thoughts out on paper like some people like to try on clothes. But I have found attempting to write about love to be a monumental undertaking. Thousands, maybe millions, of songs, books, and movies have been written on the subject in an attempt to express what it is. As I have approached this exercise in futility from various angles, I am constantly reminded of an impacting study I undertook: the reading and meditating on a book called *The Trivialization of God: The Dangerous Illusion of a Manageable Deity* by Donald McCullough (1995). To paraphrase this brilliant writer, he said that to keep trying to wrap God up in our words, explanations, and definitions was to constantly trivialize Him, bringing Him down to our size, the size of our finite brains, and thus to make Him less. That is how I feel about the subject of love. And I realize now why this book keeps jumping into my thoughts…because God IS Love. They are synonymous. The same. One subject. To confine love to any set of words is to diminish it and in doing so, lose our sense of awe.

Yet love demands acknowledgement. When it is present, we know it. When it is not present, we feel its absence. Maybe we shouldn't call it "it." For love is alive as much as any cell in our breathing bodies. Love has its own pulsating heartbeat. I have found it present in the greatest of gestures and in the tiniest. I have experienced it in places kin to palaces and in houses with dirt floors and thatched roofs. You never know where it will be and how it will surprise you. Out of all the arguments of whether love is a feeling, a decision, or a choice, I take a road less traveled, believing that we do not compartmentalize our thoughts and feelings so easily as the language suggests. If God is the source and God is love, then out of that source will come wonderful loving decisions and choices.

An Enduring Love

Once again, I am reminded that God did give Noah a blueprint for building an ark that would be a shelter, a safe place, a place of protection that would not be destroyed, no matter how weather-beaten. We have such a blueprint for how to love in scripture, and in an attempt not to trivialize love, I will say at the outset that the eyes of our hearts see dimly as through a veil. This limits us in our understanding, and our battle with the flesh limits the carrying out of this limited understanding. But God has been clear in the blueprints and in His modeling of love. It is an enduring love, a love that never fails. Never fails. If God is the source of our love, it will never fail. John says, "Beloved, let us love one another, because love is of God," (1 John 4:7a). The real thing comes from Him and that is what can last a lifetime. Words like unchangeable, unfailing, and steadfast are used over and over to describe the love of God. If you know Him, you have experienced it firsthand. May your mate experience this from you. May your love endure. May you not take your love from your beloved and give it to another. May your mate experience that your love is steadfast. May it hold in sickness and in health, in times of want and of prosperity. At the bottom line, may your love not depend on any of these circumstantial factors. May your love hold and endure just like the planks of that ark held together faithfully in times of great stress and crisis. In the I John passage, John tells us how to endure. He says, "God is love, and he who abides in love abides in God, and God in him," (1 John 4:16b).

One of the obvious places we get to observe or actually live out enduring love is when our mate is ill. In these times, they may have nothing to contribute at all, other than gratitude for our serving them. In the marriage vows we have the phrase, "in sickness and in health." I think of our soldiers wounded in combat, sometimes losing limbs. I think of women who undergo mastectomies. I think of my mother-in-law who cared for our dear Papa Joe after losing both legs to diabetes. He lived and died in his home as she showered and dressed him daily, all the while caring for all other aspects of their home. I think of mine and Gary's personal trials with his cancer diagnosis at age 32, surgeries, radiation, plastic surgeries, while we had three little boys to care for. I had a year-long bout of hepatitis contracted in Africa. I had multiple bouts with malaria. And what about enduring love in the midst of emotional challenges? I suffered with severe panic attacks for 2 years in my 30's which taxed all my energy and our finances. I remember Gary sitting up listening to me talk until the wee hours of the mornings. Some of those were on Saturday nights when he had to preach the next morning. I would look at him in the pulpit and think, "How are you standing? How are you putting sentences together?"

We say "for better or worse, richer or poorer, in sickness and in health." We may not be equipped at the time hardship comes. But God will help us lift the weight. Our friends, family, co-workers, and others will surely each take a part of the load and help us lift weights we never thought possible. This story is told over and over in a myriad of ways. Take time to think of your own times of endurance or times of friends or family members. These inspire us and call us higher.

A Growing Love

Expect an increasing love. I especially like the wording of Paul on this subject as he spoke to the Thessalonians. He said, "May the Lord make you increase and abound in love to one another," (1 Thessalonians 3:12a). When a cup is filled and keeps on being filled, it will eventually overflow. It will spill out and pour over the sides. When love grows, it is abundant and spills out. I also think of this increase being a maturing. As fruit grows, it matures and ripens and tastes better than ever. After John says that "love is from God" (our source), he says: "…if we love one another, God abides in us, and His love has been perfected in us…" (1 John 4:12). It seems to me that the passage on love in 1 Corinthians 13 really fleshes out what perfected, mature love looks like. Mature love is patient, kind, not envious, not proud, not rude, not self-seeking, not easily angered. Perfected love does not keep a ledger sheet of shortcomings and failures. It always protects, always trusts, always hopes, and always perseveres, (1 Corinthians 13:1–7). We can take our behaviors and hold them up beside these measuring sticks and see how mature we are and how perfected our love is.

We celebrate the fact that love can mature over time. An acorn is a small seed that, when nurtured well, becomes a mighty oak tree. Yet the acorn and the oak are one and the same. The acorn always has the potential, the ability, to mature into something large and magnificent, providing shelter, shade, and beauty. Much like the acorn and the oak, new love is very real. It always possesses the ability to become mature. When new love is freshly sown, it must be well nurtured. But as that love is tended, it grows strong, its roots deepen, and it becomes a mighty and powerful being capable of withstanding the temptations and pressures of external forces. As young love transforms into mature love, it transforms the lives and attitudes of the people in this mature love. It helps a heart that may be immature and selfish become a heart that is serving, selfless, and delights in the joy of another. Mature love reveals a beauty that goes beyond the surface and into the soul. Mature love becomes a place of peace, of rest, of comfort, and of bliss.

Marriages experience developmental growth stages, like that of an acorn to an oak. The young marriage must be carefully nurtured. An oak sapling is vulnerable to excessive wind and rain, to drought and insects. Like the sapling, tending to your young marriage is essential. Grow and develop your love, your marriage together. Protect it from the elements that seek to cause you harm. Learn to mature in serving one another. Take out the trash without being asked. Make a special dinner for no occasion. Find a way to put your spouse ahead of yourself. If there is a task he or she hates to do, surprise them by doing it for them. Acts of serving one another, of lowering yourself and considering your mate before yourself (when both partners do this), will deepen and strengthen the marriage tremendously. An oak sapling does not grow in one direction. But rather, as it grows stronger and taller, the roots go deeper and wider. Work together to ensure your roots go deep and are taking in the nutrients necessary to develop your marriage into a strong, impenetrable force.

Practice sacrificial love. Let's say he wants to take a walk. Go, even if it means the dishes sit a little while longer or even if you're tired. She wants to snuggle? Turn off (or record) the ball game. Sacrifice your instincts and desires to allow your spouse to feel important and a priority. It may not cost you much or it may cost a great deal. But the return on the sacrificial investment will be so much more than you put into it. Even a mature oak is not without its enemies of danger. Though the roots of your marriage may be deep, you must continue to tend to the marriage. Allowing the care to become stagnant can cause a marriage to drift and distance to creep in so slowly it is almost imperceptible until you are too far apart to call out to one another. Continue to grow in love and communication. Maturing a love is not a one-time or even a ten-time thing. It is a lifetime thing. Retired? Find new activities to do together. All talked out? Read the same book that may spark new conversations. Keep cultivating the love and communication you have both worked so long and so hard to mature.

Love is giving. The writers of the New Testament had to use the Greek word agape when searching to describe this kind of love. *Phileo*, the love between friends, didn't describe it. Neither did *eros*, referring to sensual attraction. Theologian Karl Barth, in *Church Dogmatics Vol IV Part 2*, refers to it this way, "Agape means self-giving; not the losing of oneself in the other," (1958). That has the sound of truth in it for me because I think of Jesus giving up His life for us. I think of God loving us in such a way that He gave His only Son. This giving can and often does demand sacrifice. I am in awe of the fact that God held nothing back. He gave everything. In marriage, as in parenting, the relationship will demand sacrifice. You will sacrifice your time, money, sleep, and your way. And because it is yours and you choose to give it, it will constitute a sacrifice, and the sacrifice will demonstrate love. Not only does this way of giving mean sacrifice, but it also means giving the best, giving extravagantly. When the Lord gave Moses and Aaron their blueprint for the first Passover, He told them to have each man take a lamb for his family. He said to take a lamb without defect or without blemish. When God chose a lamb, He chose a lamb without blemish. He didn't give us scraps or breadcrumbs. When you give your mate anything from tangible gifts to mowing the yard and doing the dishes, give lavishly. When you give to your mate sexually, give lavishly. When you visit the in-laws, give to your mate's family lavishly, not in gesturing fashion. No one needs your gestures any more than they desire the crumbs from your table.

The following story was told in Reader's Digest (Feb. 1988, pp. 138–141) about the difference a man made by loving his wife:

It was the story of Johnny Lingo, a man who lived in the South Pacific. The islanders all spoke highly of this man, but when it came time for him to find a wife, the people shook their heads in disbelief. In order to obtain a wife, you paid for her by giving her father cows. Four to six cows were considered a high price. But the woman Johnny Lingo chose was plain, skinny, and walked with her shoulders hunched and her head down. She was very hesitant and shy. What surprised everyone was Johnny's offer – he gave eight cows for her! Everyone chuckled about it, since they believed his father-in-law pulled one over on him.

Several months after the wedding, a visitor from the U.S. came to the islands to trade and heard the story of Johnny Lingo and his eight-cow wife. Upon meeting Johnny and his wife, the visitor was totally taken aback. This wasn't a shy, plain, and hesitant woman but one who was beautiful, poised, and confident. The visitor asked about the transformation, and Johnny Lingo's response was very simple. "I wanted an eight-cow woman, and when I paid that for her and treated her in that fashion, she began to believe that she was an eight-cow woman. She discovered she was worth more than any other woman in the islands. And what matters most is what a woman thinks about herself."

A Compelling Love

Love compels. When Paul is speaking to the church in Corinth, he says that because of the fear of the Lord, they (the disciples) are trying to "persuade men." Later in that passage, he says "if we are beside ourselves, it is for the sake of God, or if we are of sound mind, it is for you. For the love of Christ compels us," (2 Corinthians 5:11–14). It seems to me that Paul is saying we are compelled to the point that we might appear to be a little out of our minds. The word *compel* means to be forced, to be constrained. The power of love forces us. The power of love is forceful. Love is a force in itself. But the force inside love doesn't cause it to blow up like a stick of dynamite, with bits and pieces flying everywhere. No, the force of love is more like gunpowder confined in a steel casing, like a bullet. That bullet is compelled in a direction. It is moving toward something.

Love does drive us toward our mate. When we have been hurt or offended, love will constrain us, drive us, force us, compel us to forgive so that we can be restored again. Love compelled God, our Abba, toward us, His children, with unabandoned passion again and again and again. And the love of Christ constrains and compels us toward our mate again and again, restoring us to oneness. The direction is toward. The bullet casing is the love of Christ. What is inside is so powerful. What is inside is so hopeful, so healing, so lavish. Compelling love can restrain us from surrendering to temptation. The adultery sequence has a beginning of flirtation, chemical sparks, and buddings of fantasy. It can be a strong pull, but with early intervention, being compelled by love for your mate, you can stop it in the early stages. Look in the face of your mate, look into their eyes. How are they going to feel when they find out about a tryst with a co-worker or a full-blown affair? Use compelling love to move you past temptations and toward your mate.

Love is revealed in action. Noah's love for God and for his family was revealed by the many swings of his hammer, the planks he carried, and the careful attention to detail as he built the ark that would carry his family. My own husband has taught me so much about love being an active verb. As he checks my gas gauge, lifts heavy things, and makes the late night runs to the grocery, I can easily translate the language. Love brings forth, births something. Compelling love as a force contains passion and energy. When love begins to wane, passion begins to fade. Compelling love can renew your coupleship. Tap into its driving force. As a car cannot continue to move forward without a source of fuel, of power, of igniting, so love cannot continue without fuel, without power, without an igniting charge. It is like plugging into electricity. God's love compelled Him. "For God so loved the world, He gave His only begotten Son," (John 3:16a).

I see now that this chapter is really a prayer. It is the prayer of my heart that you experience this love of God. It is my prayer that this love poured into you becomes a well and that you draw from this wellspring of love deeply and often. Spill it over onto your mate lavishly, freely, forcefully, and abundantly.

"And may the Lord make you increase and abound in love to one another and to all, just as we do to you,"
(1 Thessalonians 3:12).

Conversation Starters

1. Think of a specific time when you were on the receiving end of lavish giving. Share the incident and your response with your partner.

2. Think of a message hidden in a sacrificial act of service. What is being said to the recipient? ("I care about you," "You are worth my time, my money, my sweat, my tears," "I forgive you," "I believe in you.")

3. Review the 1 Corinthians 13 passage. State your biggest challenge in regard to the attributes listed. (patient, kind, not envious, not proud, not rude, not self-seeking, not easily angered, keeps no record of wrongs).

4. Now, reread 1 Corinthians 13 again, with your own name substituted for the word, "love." (Jim is patient, Jim is kind, et al). Ask the Holy Spirit to show you areas in which you are weak and spend time in confession, repentance, and asking God to strengthen and grow you up in these areas.

5. Come up with a metaphor that, for you, represents a picture of love. (Examples: love is like an umbrella that protects one from the elements. Love is like a bridge that connects our hearts).

CHAPTER 7

Scoot Over, Noah

A Look at Intimacy

"...and they shall become one flesh."
Genesis 2:24

Scoot Over, Noah: A Look at Intimacy

T he crowded conditions in the ark must have made for necessary, constant work on the relationships. The unique situation Noah and his wife found themselves in must have demanded the highest level of communication. There must have been critical points of choice at least a hundred times a day to either move closer to each other or move further away. Intimacy is about closeness and distance. These are invisible lines, you understand, but always present nonetheless. If you could see it as concentric circles rather than in linear fashion, you would see the picture in my mind. We are in a constant flux in those circles because of our "fight or flight" mechanisms. God has placed a longing inside us to enter the center of an intimate circle with another (unless one has been called to celibacy). However, the hurts, disappointments, losses, which have resulted in fears, now may demand a lot of intentional effort to enter that circle with another. Both our fears of abandonment and engulfment will have to be faced and answered.

I believe this ultimate place of oneness is an experience of being one in body, soul, and spirit. In other words, there is physical intimacy, spiritual intimacy, and an intimacy of thoughts, wills, and emotions that will constitute the intercourse of two souls. Having all three possibilities is so rare, yet so precious, and worth the pursuit. However, it is impossible to pursue outright. You can't just wake up one morning and say, "I choose intimacy this day" or "I will be intimate." It is much more elusive than that. I believe it is more a byproduct of certain things rather than something you can attain directly. It is really a destination, this place called Intimacy. And it is reached by riding in vehicles that are going to that destination. If you say you want to go to New York, you better read the signs carefully and look for the train marked "New York." If you keep riding the train to Orlando, you are going to be terribly frustrated. There are "trains" bound for Intimacy and there are "trains" bound for Distance, Loneliness, and Ultimate Estrangement.

The Struggle for Intimacy

In the book Song of Solomon, a story of intimacy is told. We are almost taken by surprise as we overhear the conversation of the pursuant lover: "You have ravished my heart, my sister, my spouse; you have ravished my heart with one look of your eyes, with one link of your necklace. How fair is your love, my sister, my spouse! How much better than wine is your love, and the scent of your perfumes than all spices!" (Song of Solomon 4:9–10). A study of this book will reveal every element of intimacy: the spontaneity, the openness and vulnerability, the shared expression of deep thoughts and feelings, the awe and wonder, the pursuit and constant invitation to "Come."

We in this American culture are moving against a strong tide in order to lay hold of an intimate relationship. Our "American Way" is becoming daily more and more set up for privacy, individuality, anonymity, and hiddenness driven by fears of vulnerability and authenticity. Henri Nouwen writes to Fred Bratman letters which become a book, *Life of the Beloved*, concerning this trek toward intimacy with God. He says, "Becoming the Beloved means letting the truth of our Belovedness become engulfed in everything we think, say, or do. It entails a long and painful process of appropriation or better, incarnation," (1991).

Bone of my Bones, Flesh of my Flesh

It is always good to have definitions because of the specificity that leads to clear understanding. Intimacy can be broken down into four little words: in-to-me-see. This is descriptive of the sharing, openness, vulnerability, and honesty that constitute intimacy. Experiencing intimacy will result in connectedness, attachment, bonding, and feelings of oneness. For a close-up snapshot of this condition, we can go to Adam and Eve in the garden. When Adam saw Eve, he exclaimed, "This is now bone of my bones and flesh of my flesh; she shall be called Woman, because she was taken out of Man. Therefore a man shall leave his father and mother and be joined to his wife, and they shall become one flesh. And they were both naked, the man and his wife, and were not ashamed," (Genesis 2:23–25).

Without sameness (being made in God's image) and difference (male and female), there could be no intimacy. They were one and yet two, separate, and distinct. This is the fabric out of which intimacy can be woven. Two distinct persons, equal in value, with bone-deep emotional, spiritual, physical relatedness, totally transparent without fear of being known; that is the picture of intimacy. We can therefore begin to use the Bible's graphic image of marital intimacy to describe our own condition: "covered with fig leaves" and "naked." Isn't it interesting that they didn't even know they were naked until the fall? Scripture says, "Then the eyes of both of them were opened, and they knew that they were naked," (Genesis 3:7a). Notice how sin and the fall brought in the elements of fear, guilt, and shame, which led to hiding. Fear, guilt, and shame bind and hold hostage. But thank

God, we haven't been left there, due to Christ's shed blood on the cross.

An Environment of Safety

I said earlier that there are vehicles that lead to Intimacy and vehicles that lead in the opposite direction. First of all, I believe an *atmosphere of safety* is a bottom line necessity for the state of intimacy. Paul told husbands to "love your wife, just as Christ also loved the church and gave Himself for her." He went on to say, "So husbands ought to love their own wives as their own bodies; he who loves his wife loves himself," (Ephesians 5:25, 28). It goes without saying that all forms of verbal, emotional, and physical abuse should be absent in a marriage. Unfortunately, many people have to live with such threats.

Emotional abuse consists of things like belittling, discounting, paybacks, punishment by withholding, and the silent treatment. It can be very evil and sometimes quite subtle. Verbal abuse is common in times of anger and carries a destructive punch as surely as physical abuse. Name-calling and cursing introduce a level of violence into the relationship. Throwing objects, slamming doors, and cornering your mate are all acts that will cut so deeply into trust that it can take months to restore.

Kudzu is an invasive plant prominent throughout the South. It grows rapidly and will overtake stationary objects, including trees, buildings, or abandoned vehicles. It kills the vegetation on which it grows by choking out the sunlight. Much like kudzu, possessiveness and abuse can drive away the needed sustenance for growth in a marriage. Paul said, "Let all bitterness, wrath, anger, clamor, and evil speaking be put away from you, with all malice," (Ephesians 4:31).

Of course, these acts of destruction can be performed by the husband or the wife. You can see that the idea of safety involves trust based on consistency and reliability. It is disrupted by acts of aggression, unexpected behavior, and a third element: neglect. Neglect means the person is just not there in legitimately expected ways. I will never forget a story told by a client of a miserable night of stomach upset to the point of her lying down on the bathroom floor. Her husband got up and dressed for work, came into the bathroom, brushed his teeth, combed his hair, and walked out without a word. Neglect can come in much more common ways, most notably through busyness and life's distractions.

When we are born into this world, I believe we have two questions, "Will anyone out there love me?" and "Does anybody care?" I believe these questions come to the forefront again as we stand at the altar: "Will you love me?" "Will you care?" The resounding yes's must come time after time in order to tie the knots in our safety net. But the point is, the lack of safety in any of these arenas will diminish, and in some cases make impossible, the possibility of intimacy. But Paul's instructions, "And be kind to one another, tenderhearted…" (Ephesians 4:32a) will lead to a place of trust and nurturing. Do you care?

Sexuality and Sensuality

Our Creator made us wonderfully and fearfully, so the Psalmist says. Part of that design was to give to couples physical touch and sexuality to enhance their intimacy. Years ago, I put together a talk for teens entitled, "God's not a dirty old man." I talked about our God creating sex from a place of holiness and righteousness. Sex is an amazing gift!

So here we are today, finding ourselves in a deluge of sexuality and sensuality, yet in a cultural crisis around intimacy. It seems that a couple who have tied the marital knot would then experience the freedom afforded them. In a safe, loving environment, why are so many struggling to maintain a meaningful sexual relationship? And I do mean struggling. One set of issues surrounds prior sexual abuse, shame, and a host of triggers surrounding sex from prior experiences. Early molestation, date rapes, and degrading experiences, can all have backlash later in life and prevent healthy sexuality. Also, some men and women are afflicted with having little or no sex drive, or experience pain during sex. I am pleading with you not to let these problems go unattended. Please seek help for you and for your mate. And do not quit until you have found help physically or mentally that has restored your sexual health.

The biggest and most deceptive enemy to healthy sexuality within a marriage today is, of course, pornography. The accessibility and affordability have given rise to the enormity of this problem, which grows by the day. I was in a Summit conference on sex addiction a while back in Atlanta and the speaker announced that a tsunami was coming. My colleague and I just looked at each other, saying with our eyes, "How can it get any worse?" But he proceeded over the next two days to inform us as to how it is going to get worse and the specifics were frightening. The flares are being raised in our profession around the inability of sex addicts to attach in any meaningful way after hours and hours of objectifying a man or woman in their private acting out. It doesn't take Einstein to figure out that a normal person is not going to measure up to the heights of stimulation provided through the internet, whose gamut is endless, not to mention endlessly perverted. I beg you to stop. Give your partner a chance to have an intimate, loving partner. Give your partner a chance to BE an intimate, loving partner. Be honest, with your partner as well as with yourself. Please get professional help, whether on your own or with your partner.

And lastly, let me say to the couples who are now dependent on pornographic material in order to perform sexually with each other: make your way. Make your way to something healthy and pure. Restore pure love to your relationship and your relationship with God. I truly believe that the Edenic experience is available today, due to the removal of fear, shame, and guilt. This work was done on the cross. Intimacy is available. Restore the beauty to what God created and provided in this area.

The Eye of the Beholder

My favorite word in the marriage vows is *cherish*. There is something so sweet and tender about this word that encompasses the concepts of honoring and prizing your mate. Prizing is a term borrowed from child development terminology, for it is so important for a child to have the experience of being prized. Let's face it. I think that feeling is experienced once more in the eye of the beholder. Paul, in Ephesians 5:29, goes right on to say, "For no one ever hated his own flesh, but nourishes and cherishes it, just as the Lord does the church." In an atmosphere of nourishment and being cherished, intimacy can grow and flourish. Things like listening, affirming, honoring, and respecting are all going to be critical elements of cherishing your mate. These are vehicles headed toward greater intimacy. Deliberate attention needs to be paid, though, for it is so easy to slip into taking a person for granted just by getting used to having them there.

In today's world, with so much pulling and tugging, staying in tune with your mate will take lots of focused intention. You will have to build rituals of "good mornings," and kisses and hugs, and "please's," and "thank-you's." Remember eye contact, getting your message through the window of the soul into the center of the heart. Remember cuddling, hand-holding, spooning, smiles, and Eskimo kisses. Remember date nights and walks in the park. Remember flowers and chocolate-covered strawberries. Remember heads bowed and praying together. Remember singing in the shower. Remember laughter. To lose the sense of awe, the sense of wonder toward your mate, is to lose such a precious, mysterious commodity. If you are reading this material as a refresher course, step back and take a fresh look at this person God created. You and your Chosen One are fearfully and wonderfully made in the image of our God. Their very being shouts, "Precious cargo. Handle with care!"

The Heart of Restoration

I want to keep emphasizing again and again, that just as God gave Noah instructions that caused the ark to float and the people in it to live, He has given a blueprint for marriage that will absolutely work in our day. God, Himself, modeled this pursuit of intimacy for us. God's love affair with Israel is portrayed for us over and over. However, it was much more than an affair. It was a covenant relationship and in it, He exhibited the last vehicle I want to point to. That is the vehicle of *forgiveness*, His constant pursuit to restore intimacy whenever it was broken. No other book portrays this better for me that Hosea. God clearly states all the ways that His Beloved, Israel, has been unfaithful while He always maintained His faithfulness. After a whole litany of their blatant failures, including that she (Israel) even forgot Him, He immediately says, "Therefore, behold, I will allure her, will bring her into the wilderness and speak comfort to her. I will give her vineyards from there and the Valley of Achor as a door of hope; she shall sing there, as in the days of her youth," (Hosea 2:14–15a). Later in that passage, God says, "I will betroth you to Me forever; Yes, I will betroth you to Me in righteousness and justice, in lovingkindness and mercy I will betroth you to Me in faithfulness," (Hosea 2:19–20). The fact that this passage starts with "therefore" is just mind boggling to me in lieu of the fact that God just stated a list of ways Israel betrayed Him. But He is God, and this is how deep and wide His love is! Following that, His intentions to call her away so He can comfort her, all the ways He desires to provide for her, underlining His loyalty, and wrapping it all in love and mercy, far outweigh what she deserves. This is God's blueprint for safety, cherishing, and restoration in times of failure. Following these principles will allow for the creation and flourishing of an intimate relationship.

"I am my beloved's and my beloved is mine; he feeds his flock among the lilies,"
(Song of Solomon 6:3).

Conversation Starters

1. It was declared in this lesson that only persons considered "equal in value" could experience intimacy. Why do you think this is true or not true?

2. Imagine that inside yourself, you have 7 rooms. How many rooms have you allowed your loved one in at this point?

3. Of the three elements that entered in the fall: fear, shame, and guilt, which do you feel binds you the most when it comes to the challenges of vulnerability?

4. Please complete this sentence: "The fig leaves I have used to hide behind in the past are…" (Examples are physical attractiveness, being the expert, shyness, being the joker, etc.)

CHAPTER 8

Two by Two

Male and Female Differences

"I will praise You, for I am fearfully and wonderfully made. Marvelous are Your works,"
(Psalms 139:14).

Two by Two: Male and Female Differences

Noah received his instructions directly from God. It is to our benefit to note the specificity with which God's instructions were given. Noah was told, "And of every living thing of all flesh you shall bring two of every sort into the ark, to keep them alive with you; they shall be male and female," (Genesis 6:19). No doubt, all of us have seen the artists' rendition of the animals lined up to go into the ark. This is a picture of God's creativity, His love for color, size, and smells. Each one is valued and prized by his Maker. And God has left this imprint of variety on us, male and female, both alike and different. Each person is an original work of art.

Regarding human attributes, the sources of our differences come on many distinct levels. Our Creator leaves His unique mark on us, to be sure. Most scientists do not hold to the "blank slate" theory, but rather believe that we are born with predisposed personality traits. These will influence our personal responses to stimuli, particularly whether we will move towards, away, or against those stimuli. (Horney, 1945). Each of us over time will develop our own patterns of responding emotionally and intellectually to life. The most basic building blocks of our differences are encoded in our physiology and anatomy, of course. Here are a few of those: While performing tasks, men and women have been shown to utilize different parts of their brains. This results in a man's ability to compartmentalize and simplify tasks, and a woman to provide more attention to the relational aspects at hand and the ability to multitask. How the male and female brains process neurochemicals like serotonin, testosterone, estrogen, and oxytocin, all influence the differences in the needs and responses. Emotionally, women usually have high needs for safety and security, likely connected to their child-bearing roles. She looks for consistency and predictability and loves to "know" the plan. The male may be just fine creating the plan along the way. For a more in depth outline of these differences, I would point to an article from February 2014 in **Psychology Today**, entitled, "Brain Differences between Genders" by Dr. Gregory Jantz.

Our needs and responses are influenced by our different physiologies, how we are shaped by genetics, and by the environment of our family of origin, including their beliefs and patterns. Each family has its own language by which the world is coded. We are taught how to hang "price tags" on circumstances: "This is good, that is bad;" "This is weak, that is strong." The modeling and teaching we receive are powerful teachers and become reference points in life. Last but definitely not least is the influence of birth order in the family. Here is a very general overview of the influence of those positions: the first-born child is a rule-follower and wants to do it "right." They usually become responsible adults and develop into independent leaders. They are at the most risk of becoming workaholics. Second-born children usually become keen observers, really desiring for people to make peace and get along. They often develop skill sets of mediators and peacekeepers. Third children enter the world with less voting power and tend to stay more outside of the family circle and learn to entertain themselves. Fourth children usually see what is needed by the family when they arrive on the scene and learn to provide it. If they sense the family needs to lighten up, they will provide the laughter. If the family has a core of shame, they may attempt to make the family proud. An only child, of course, may bear the task of providing parts of all these roles and is at risk of becoming over responsible and not sure where they end and others begin.

Challenges to Establishing Oneness

In premarital work, the couple can be seen as two puzzle pieces. How will they fit together? For instance, if the female is a traditional first-born leader and she is marrying a third-born who has learned to hold back and observe, they can face critical points around her expectations of wanting him to lead. This comes up fairly often. The female often has expectations of someone to lead her or take care of her. However, she may face her own conflicts around wanting to be independent and the fears of "being controlled." These two pieces may have a tough time "fitting together."

We are usually attracted initially by the differences exhibited by individuals. In some ways, the old adage that opposites attract is true. It is also true, however, the things that initially attract us to one another may later be the very qualities that repel. The woman who is so impressed that her husband is disciplined enough to save for a honeymoon in Hawaii, may at some point resent his thriftiness and feel controlled by his bent towards saving. The man who may be drawn to a woman who is organized, neat, and structured may later be asking her, "Where's your spontaneity? Can't you lighten up a little?" These potential challenges lie within our differences and how we learn to handle them will be crucial to the marriage.

I have tried to establish that differences will be present. Many times they are the initial attractors, but at some point the tide may turn and you may find it challenging to keep *appreciating* those differences. In fact, there is a strong bent in us to try to make people over in *our* own image. If they are like me, somehow it validates that I am *right* or at least *okay.* How we handle this challenge is pivotal. I believe there are three main pillars to relationships: love, trust, and respect. The pillar at risk here is *respect*. To keep a sense of awe and honoring toward your mate takes a deliberate choice. Couples who do not successfully navigate these rough waters will sink to nagging and criticizing. Constant nagging, bickering, and criticism are like dry rot that will severely damage and eventually destroy your marriage ark. The spirit of condemnation and judgment can slip in through the door of differences all too easily. The result here is dishonor and disrespect. If the descent continues, each person will feel the rejection, not just for what they did, but for *who they are*. One can be a saver, the other a spender; one social, the other more introverted; one can love sports, the other can prefer shopping; one can thrive in order, the other in chaos.

When Noah had squeaks in the hinges of his door, I am sure that he got out his trusty oil and applied it to the hinges. When the relationship is developing squeaks over differences, we, too, must reach for the "oil" and make its application. David Augsburger, in his book *Sustaining Love*, says this about differences: "Differences first attract, then irritate, then frustrate, then illuminate, and finally may unite us. Those traits intrigue in courtship, amuse in early marriage, begin to change in time and infuriate in the conflicts of middle marriage; but maturation begins to change their meaning and the uniqueness of the other person becomes prized," (1988). What Augsburger is describing here is a process and we must enter that process with our oil so that the outcome he has described will be achieved.

God has instructed us regarding the ingredients for the "oil" of relationships. The whole premise of this study is that

Noah was delivered from the fate of death by drowning through his careful listening and obedience to God's instructions. So, as we search for how to navigate through potentially dangerous relationship waters, we must look for His instructions.

Oiling the Hinges of Relationship

I would ask you to consider several ingredients constituting the oil mixture with which we can treat the squeaky hinges of marriage. The foremost ingredient I would name is *humility*, descriptive of an attitude, a stance of heart to be taken toward your mate. Jesus addressed it in the Sermon on the Mount: "Judge not, that you be not judged. For with what judgment you judge, you will be judged; and with the same measure you use, it will be measured back to you. And why do you look at the speck in your brother's eye, but do not consider the plank in your own eye?" (Matthew 7:1–3). Judgment is the fruit of arrogance and refraining from judgment is the fruit of humility.

Humility would see a fault in another and in the same moment, become aware of similar faults in one's own character. Humility would not demand change as a tyrant demands subservience. Instead, it would help the person change what they desire to change. It doesn't say, "Here is my vision for you. Please adopt it." It says instead, "What is your vision? How can I support you in reaching it?" In writing about differences, James Fairfield said, "How arrogant of me to think I could shape another human being! How humble it makes me to realize that I need to yield to another and thereby be changed!" (1977). Let your differences from your mate be a unifying force, instead of a divisive one. Celebrate and be grateful the two of you do not think exactly alike. You are each stronger and better for the other one and can glean a better life when a second perspective on an issue is *respectfully* presented.

An equally important ingredient in this oil mixture is *mercy*. Jesus was a man of mercy. He blessed the merciful. David asked twice in Psalms 41, "O Lord, be merciful to me." As we desire God to have mercy on us, may we learn to apply mercy to others. Giving mercy instead of demanding perfection will build a bridge in the relationship. Mercy speaks of love that is unconditional. Mercy speaks God's language. When God was working through Hosea to exemplify His love for Israel, He instructed Hosea to say, "Mercy be shown." In the language of marriage, God said, "I will betroth you to Me forever; yes, I will betroth you to Me in righteousness and justice, in lovingkindness and mercy." He ends His plea with a promise, "And I will have mercy on her who had not obtained mercy," (Hosea 2:19, 23). Ask yourself, "Am I merciful? Do I give grace and mercy to my spouse?" If you cannot answer "yes," consider how you can show mercy. When mercy, when unconditional love, is shown consistently, change often follows and mercy is often reciprocated. Giving mercy may be a catalyst to healing.

They grew up with different socioeconomic, cultural, and even religious backgrounds. The marriage examples they experienced in their families of origin were polar opposite. No computer algorithm would have ever matched them. Yet Luke and Kate knew they belonged together. While they certainly had things in common, their differences were many. It would have been easy to bicker at every turn. He could have been dominant and belittling, as he witnessed growing up. She could have diminished his upbringing and thus, his abilities as a man. But they work to allow their differences to be complimentary instead of oppositional. She admires his strength and determination in allowing his past to motivate him forward instead of repeating it. He embraces her traditional background and desire to build a drama-free home. Consider a puzzle...if all the pieces were identical, they could never fit together to create a beautiful picture. Luke's and Kate's differences became their strengths. She tries to give him unconditional acceptance and love in a way he had never before experienced. He helps her have more patience and encourages her. While their minds do not often arrive at the same solution to issues, they work hard to listen and give value to the other's ideas instead of insisting on "rightness." She values his analytical and common sense solutions while he admires her creative bend. And often, the end result is better than either could have arrived at on their own.

Rewards of Living in Oneness

When marriage partners begin with this mixture, humility and mercy, they will be able to make it through the challenging passages of the relationship waters. Critical pitfalls of criticism and finger-pointing may thus be avoided. In continuing the practice of humility and mercy, partners will be living out Paul's encouragement in Ephesians 4:1–3: "I...beseech you to walk worthy of the calling with which you were called, with all lowliness and gentleness, with longsuffering, bearing with one another in love, endeavoring to keep the unity of the Spirit in the bond of peace." The result will be building up rather than tearing down. Each mate will feel cherished, valued, and appreciated.

Paul used the illustration of the different parts of the body working together as a unit. He paints a vivid word picture when he asks to imagine the whole body as an eye. He then asks where would the sense of hearing be? Or if the whole body were an ear, where would the sense of smell be? As each of us brings our different "senses" to the relationship, life is multiplied and enhanced. Our different opinions, likes and dislikes, and personal views may fill in missing pieces. Back to Paul's metaphors: if all was an eye, where would the hearing be. If we truly understood this concept, I believe we would welcome, delight in, and embrace our differences. The insecure person, however, will see it as threatening and ultimately, something to be squelched.

The passage in 1 Corinthians continues with the body analogy: "And the eye cannot say to the hand, 'I have no need of you'; nor again the head to the feet, 'I have no need of you.' No, much rather, those members of the body which seem to be weaker are necessary. And those members of the body which we think to be less honorable, on these we bestow great honor," (1 Corinthians 12:21–23a). When anyone different than us is treated with honor and seen as indispensable, our relatedness will be strengthened.

We are always led through the Holy Spirit back to the purposes of unity and peace—the two remaining one. Maybe this chapter could best be summed up through Paul's admonition in Romans 14:19: "Therefore let us pursue the things which make for peace and the things by which one may edify another."

"So God created man in his image, in the image of God he created him; male and female he created them,"
(Genesis 1:27).

Conversation Starters

1. Have each partner circle the characteristic which they are most like:

   a. The quiet type
      Very verbally expressive

   b. Neat, with attention to detail
      Sloppy and unorganized

   c. Bargain hunter, dollar store variety
      High Quality Shopper

   d. Bookworm
      TV addict

   e. Planning is the best way
      Spontaneity is best

   f. Logical reasoning
      Respond from feeling

2. Have each person share their responses and decide which of these differences presently causes them the most difficulty in the relationship.

3. Ask what attitude of the heart each person thinks they personally need to adopt in order to apply "oil" to the squeaky hinges of the relationship.

4. Think about individually, and discuss as a couple, if there is a style in the list that may not only cause problems with others, but also within yourself. If so, how could it be changed?

CHAPTER 9

The Ship Called Grace

"Let your gentleness be known to all men."
Philippians 4:5

The Ship Called Grace

I feel pretty certain that if Noah had time before the rains came, he would have painted the letters on the side of the ark: G-R-A-C-E. For it was by God's grace that this family was spared in the midst of chaos. I feel certain, too, that daily applications of grace had to be made toward one another inside that ship on a myriad of occasions during their voyage. Grace oiled the hinges of the relationships on a regular basis. For within such close confinement, a kind of magnifying-glass syndrome sets in. In such close quarters, the faults and shortcomings must be revealed.

Forbearing One Another in Love

And so it is with marriage. When a couple gets a closer look within daily living, there is no place to hide. The warts and blemishes begin to show. What we do at that juncture is quite crucial in the scheme of marriage. I believe if we choose one of the grace-filled principles, that of *forbearing*, big dividends will be paid. Paul said to the Ephesians that he "beseeched" them to "walk worthy of the calling with which you were called, with all lowliness and gentleness, with longsuffering, bearing with one another in love, endeavoring to keep the unity of the Spirit in the bond of peace." (Ephesians 4:1–3).

I have heard that the word *forbear* means literally "to put up with." You can negotiate, ask nicely, make requests, and all sorts of tactics to influence change in your mate. (And I highly recommend all of the above.) They can be healthy means for communicating your likes and dislikes. But in the end, there will always be a need for grace to fill in the cracks of your relationship, a need to forbear some things that don't readily change. A story was told to me once as truth, yet to this day I don't know if it really happened. I was told that this woman got so tired of nagging her husband to pick up his socks and underwear that he came home one day only to find what he had left lying around now nailed to the floor!

This makes a pretty good point. When we get tired of applying grace, we usually next use a hammer. This hammer is normally labeled "Criticism." Gottman says "The first cascade a couple hits as they tumble down the marital rapids is comprised of 'The Four Horsemen of the Apocalypse,' four disastrous ways of interacting that sabotage your attempts to communicate with your partner." He names criticism, contempt, defensiveness, and stonewalling. He says as these patterns become more and more entrenched, the couple focuses increasingly on the negatives. "As each horseman arrives, he paves the way for the next and insidiously overrides a marriage that started out full of promise." (1994). I think this was the concept the author was relaying in the book of Matthew when he spoke of the speck and the plank. He said, "And why do you look at the speck in your brother's eye, but do not consider the plank in your own eye? Or how can you say to your brother, 'Let me remove the speck from your eye,' and look, a plank is in your own eye? Hypocrite! First remove the plank from your own eye, and then you will see clearly to remove the speck from your brother's eye," (Matthew 7:3–5).

I have this theory that says, "With every interaction, I have an opportunity to participate in the healing of this person, or I have an opportunity of participating in the further tearing of their wounds." Adopting the passage from Isaiah 61 as part of your vision for marriage would be an incredible mission statement:

He has sent Me to heal the brokenhearted, to proclaim liberty to the captives, and the opening of the prison to those who are bound; to proclaim the acceptable year of the Lord, and the day of vengeance of our God; to comfort all who mourn, to console those who mourn in Zion, to give them beauty for ashes, and the oil of joy for mourning, (verses 1b–3a).

As a mate, you possess a tube of ointment that can be applied to hurt places. You are in a unique position to "bind up," to "proclaim," to "comfort," and to "bestow." The question is not will you or won't you do these things. Rather, the question is **what** will you proclaim and **what** will you bestow?

Wisdom and the Application of Grace

It takes wisdom and discernment to know when to address a problem and when to let it go. The wrong decision can lead to shoving something under the rug. Do this enough and eventually you are walking around a mountain in the middle of your living room floor. Another key is to recognize the difference between suppressing something and truly letting it go. I remember one night being very tired but still needing to make a trip to the grocery store for some desperately required items. Gary in his gallantry came in on a white horse to save the day and offered to go to the store for me. When he returned, there were several generic brand items he had picked up in place of the name brands I had listed. I don't like generic brands for certain recipes. He, on the other hand, thought he was being a smart shopper and saving us money. I was about to get on one of those four horses and ride, ready to criticize his choices and set him straight on how these dishes wouldn't taste quite the same. Instead, I suddenly felt as if God Himself bridled my tongue. I saw immediately how ungrateful I was about to be and went straight to my husband, hugged him, and thanked him for being such a great husband and caring for me. If only I could make that choice all of the time. Grace covers, grace overlooks, grace forbears, grace sees a bigger picture.

I am not encouraging a resigned, stuff-your-feelings, defeated acceptance here, but an acceptance that embraces your mate with expectancy and excitement. If your grace-filled acceptance is not genuine, the gaps in your relationship will be filled with rejection. Your mate's companions will eventually be fear and insecurity. When you realize you are nitpicking your mate, let that realization be a turning point. Paul said, "Let nothing be done through selfish ambition or conceit, but in lowliness of mind let each esteem others better than himself," (Philippians 2:3). The choice to overlook is one we will all appreciate when the shoe is on the other foot. How many times are *we* in need of God's grace in just one day?

The Receiving End of Tender Mercies

One story in the Bible really stands out for me in fleshing out this concept: The Prodigal Son. When the son had squandered his inheritance and made his way back home, the father certainly had the right to lecture and point out every failure to the son. But you know the story: "his father saw him and had compassion, and ran and fell on his neck and kissed him. And the son said to him, 'Father, I have sinned against heaven and in your sight, and am no longer worthy to be called your son.' But the father said to his servants, 'Bring out the best robe and put it on him, and put a ring on his hand and sandals on his feet. And bring the fatted calf here and kill it…'" (Luke 15:20b–23a). I desire to be on the receiving end of this kind of tender mercy and grace. My hope and prayer for myself and for you is that we may learn to be on the *giving end* of this kind of grace.

We have within our grasp many avenues to fully give grace. We can give with the words from our mouths, of course. We can say grace-filled things like, "I could have done the same thing; I understand because I'm human too; I forgive you." We can give grace with a touch: a squeeze of the hand, a touch to the face, a hug, a kiss. We can give grace with our attitude: to respect, to admire, to appreciate, to feel gratitude, to esteem one another highly. We can sometimes express grace most of all with our silence: what we choose to let go, the things we choose to overlook, the failures and shortcomings we do not point out. It is beyond human comprehension that the Father in the story of the Prodigal Son skipped over his offenses and went straight to the ring, the robe, and the sandals. What a deep source of love, mercy, and grace that decides to go this route. What a rich gift. What an amazing grace!

Sending Forth the Dove: Ministering to Your Mate

So, as Noah's story ends, we find the storms subsiding and the ark at rest safely sitting again on firm, dry land. Scripture records that "And he waited yet another seven days, and again he sent the dove out from the ark. Then the dove came to him in the evening and behold, a freshly plucked olive leaf was in her mouth; and Noah knew that the waters had receded from the earth!" (Genesis 8:10–11). What jubilation the people inside the ark must have experienced when it was apparent that there was finally dry land! The messenger, a bird that has come to represent gentleness and purity, was bearing an olive leaf. The olive branch has taken on its own symbolism over time, one of peace and in this particular case, an emblem of reconciliation between God and the earth.

It has been my contention for a number of years that on your wedding day, you take up a calling of God. I believe you stand called into the ministry that will be your highest calling in life. In this relationship, you will have opportunity like no other, to be a part of ministering to another person on this earth. Will you be a vessel of gentleness and purity and goodwill, bearing, as it were, an olive branch between your lips, anxious to bring peace and reconciliation?

There are many scriptures admonishing us to be salt and light on the earth and encouraging us how to speak, act, and adjust our attitudes after the likeness of Christ. For the purposes of this lesson, I want to take a chapter from the Bible and see what can be gleaned for the life of a minister. This is an important equipping chapter for this concept and I want to work this concept into the soil of our hearts. I will paraphrase somewhat to apply this scripture specifically for marriage.

You have probably heard, like I have, about the man who told the preacher, "Now you've quit preaching and gone to meddling," when things got too personal. That's how I feel about this passage. After the years of hearing many sordid details in people's personal lives, I would ask you, beg you, to consider the huge prices paid in relationships where this passage has been ignored. Men and women, please don't walk like the world walks: in lust, pornography, the boys and girls-night-out in the tradition of strip clubs.

The Call to Unity

If we are called to walk alongside another person on the path and hope to make that path, there is no better body of scripture to tell us the *how* of it than Ephesians 4. Remember the theme of this book is that, by following God's directions, our ark can also survive turbulent times. The instructions in Ephesians 4 are like picking up the blueprints and reminding ourselves about the size of the planks, remembering the pitch that seals the planks. So in summary of building this ark, would you pay close attention as we draw to an end, the encouragement to build your marriage with great intention and detail.

Paul says to *walk worthy of the calling (to marriage).* So remember the holiness of the institution conceived in the mind of God. "*walk with lowliness and gentleness, with long-suffering, bearing with one another in love, endeavoring to keep unity...in the bond of peace,*" (Ephesians 4:1–3). What if, in the middle of feeling irritated that John left his smelly sports socks lying right there in the middle of the bedroom floor or his dirty dishes on the table one more time...what if Sue could remember this passage? What different attitudes and potential actions might she take in light of these words? What if Hannah has laundry piled on the bed and Sean can't even get in it when he is exhausted? And now she is in the kids' bedroom, reading to them before she tucks them in and Sean is left to fold the clothes himself? What if? What if Sean remembers these instructions, how might the evening go differently? Will these couples be more unified or more distant?

Let's keep reading: "that we should no longer be children, tossed to and fro and carried by every wind," (Ephesians 4:14). Instead of completing that with wind of doctrine, what if for our purposes, we thought of being in the ark and the winds are blowing hard and the boat is rocking? How could Bill and Teresa in the midst of adversity, not turn into children? How could they stand strong in their resolve, their faith, and their commitments in times of frustration and disappointments? Paul goes on to say, "*grow up in all things into Him who is the head – Christ,*" (verse 15). I like a word picture of a mature husband in Chuck Swindoll's book, Growing Strong in the Seasons of Life. He says, "we're talking roots and wings. A husband's love is strong enough to reassure, yet unthreatened enough to release. Tight enough to embrace, yet loose enough to enjoy. Magnetic enough to hold, yet magnanimous enough to allow for flight...with an absence of jealousy as others applaud her accomplishments and admire her competency," (1983).

A friend of ours in New Zealand, a seasoned veteran in prayer, once sent us a letter with a picture he had drawn inside. He said he as was praying, he saw a picture in his mind of Gary and me represented as two trees by a stream of water. As the trees grew taller side by side, their branches became interwoven. I have taken hope and comfort in that picture through the years.

And Paul's closing instructions in this passage, "*Put away lying and speak truth (to your spouse)...Be angry but do not sin. Do not let the sun go down on your wrath...Let no corrupt word proceed out of your mouth, but what is good for necessary edification, that it may impart grace (to your spouse)...Let all bitterness, wrath, anger, clamor, and evil speaking be away from you...and be* **kind to one another, tenderhearted, forgiving one another, even as God in Christ forgave you...**(verses 25–32). Paul gets incredibly practical at the end of the chapter, doesn't he? Speak the truth, be careful with your anger, don't hold on to it, speak things that build up. And while you're at it, speak it with kindness. Following these principles would indeed guarantee safe arrival for your ark.

There is no higher calling than ministering to your mate. There is no brighter light set on top of a hill than a healthy, godly marriage. May you build carefully. May you build with God's blueprint in hand. May you be diligent and faithful in guiding your marriage ark through the storms. May your ark be a safe place of refuge and protection to your entire family. May you arrive on dry land with thankful hearts. May you celebrate when you see the green of the olive branch.

"And God is able to make all grace abound toward you, that you, always having sufficiency in all things, may have an abundance for every good work,"
(2 Corinthians 9:8).

"He who says he abides in Him ought himself also to walk just as He walked,
(1 John 2:6).

Conversation Starters

1. Stop and check within yourselves to see if, in your personal live, you are living more performance-based or grace-based. How do you know?

2. In the story of the prodigal son, what would you have done as the father, given your answer to question 1?

3. Consider the following: your mate is perpetually late whenever you are getting ready to go somewhere. This has caused a lot of embarrassment to you, especially when meals or meeting other people are involved. This has been going on for some time. At this critical juncture, you decide to...

4. Now, stop and take a mental and emotional snapshot of the above scene. Take this picture at exactly 20 minutes of waiting. What are you thinking? What are you feeling? Would you remain "open" or start shutting down? Would you remain "connected" or become "disconnected?"

5. What will be your greatest challenge in the context of this lesson, based on your personal history?

6. Paul admonishes us to walk with all lowliness, gentleness, long-suffering, and bearing with one another. Why do you think he refers to this as a worthy way to walk? Why is it important to walk in a worthy way?

7. What will your personal challenges be to walk in this worthy way? What will be required of you in order to change in your deficit areas?

About the Author

Margaret A. Phillips, M.S. holds a master's degree in clinical psychology. She is a clinical fellow in the American Association of Marriage and Family Therapists and has over 30 years of experience in private practice as a licensed Marriage and Family Therapist. She lives in Nashville, TN with her husband, where they enjoy their children and 13 grandchildren.

References

The American Heritage Dictionary. Turtleback Books, 2012.

Augsburger, David W. *Sustaining Love: Healing & Growth in the Passages of Marriage.* Ventura, CA, U.S.A.: Regal Books, 1988.

Barth, Karl. *Church Dogmatics Volume IV The Doctrine of Reconciliation Part 2.* New York, T&T Clark International, 1958.

Fairfield, James G. T. *When You Don't Agree.* Scottdale, PA: Herald Press, 1977.

Gottman, John Mordechai., and Nan Silver. *Why Marriages Succeed or Fail: What You Can Learn from the Breakthrough Research to Make Your Marriage Last.* New York: Simon & Schuster, 1994.

Horney, Karen, MD. *Our Inner Conflicts. A Constructive Theory of Neurosis.* New York, W. W. Norton Company, 1945.

Howe, Reuel L. *The Miracle of Dialogue.* Greenwich, CT: Seabury Press, 1963.

Jantz, Gregory, PhD. "Brain Differences between Genders." *Psychology Today*, February 2014.

Ketterman, Grace H. *Verbal Abuse.* Ann Arbor, MI: Servant Publications, 1992.

Lerner, Harriet, PhD. *The Dance of Anger: A Woman's Guide to Changing the Patterns of Intimate Relationships.* New York, Harper & Row, 1985.

McCullough, Donald W. *The Trivialization of God: The Dangerous Illusion of a Manageable Deity.* Colorado Springs, CO: NavPress, 1995.

McGerr, Patricia. "The Eight-Cow Wife." *Reader's Digest*, February 1988, 138-141.

Nouwen, Henri J. M. *Life of the Beloved: Spiritual Living in a Secular World.* New York, Crossroad Publishing Company, 1992.

Nouwen, Henri J. M. *The Return of the Prodigal Son: A Story of Homecoming.* New York, Doubleday, 1992.

Pipher, Mary Bray. *The Shelter of Each Other: Rebuilding Our Families.* New York: G.P. Putnam's Sons, 1996.

Swindoll, Charles R. *Growing Strong in the Seasons of Life.* Portland, Or.: Multnomah Press, 1983.

Townsend, John. *Hiding From Love: How to Change the Withdrawal Patterns That Isolate and Imprison You.* Colorado Springs, CO: NavPress, 1991.

CPSIA information can be obtained
at www.ICGtesting.com
Printed in the USA
LVOW08s1747220617
539023LV00002B/535/P